"A fascinating account of the realities, warts and all, of everyday life on a housing estate in Dublin ... a remarkable book and a welcome addition to the literature on social housing estates."
Tracey Shildrick, Newcastle University

"An excellent book that both theorises and tells the vital story of the reality and importance of class and public housing – how vital public housing is, the identities formed around it, the strength of community, but also the challenges and structural inequalities that residents face on a daily basis. An essential read for anyone interested in public and social housing, class and inequalities."
Rory Hearne, Maynooth University

IT'S NOT WHERE YOU LIVE, IT'S HOW YOU LIVE

Class and Gender Struggles in a Dublin Estate

John Bissett

First published in Great Britain in 2023 by

Policy Press, an imprint of
Bristol University Press
University of Bristol
1-9 Old Park Hill
Bristol
BS2 8BB
UK
t: +44 (0)117 374 6645
e: bup-info@bristol.ac.uk

Details of international sales and distribution partners are available at
policy.bristoluniversitypress.co.uk

British Library Cataloguing in Publication Data
A catalogue record for this book is available from the British Library

ISBN 978-1-4473-6821-2 hardcover
ISBN 978-1-4473-6822-9 paperback
ISBN 978-1-4473-6823-6 ePub
ISBN 978-1-4473-6824-3 ePdf

Cover design: Liam Roberts
Front cover image: unsplash/keithcamilleri
Bristol University Press and Policy Press use environmentally responsible print partners.
Printed and bound in Great Britain by CMP, Poole

Contents

Acknowledgements

A deep debt of gratitude is due to all of the following: to my partner and soul mate, Grainne, and to our three children, Laoise, Kara and Zoe, thanks for everything.

I would like to thank a number of people and groups without whom this project and book would, more than likely, not have got to publication. I have been lucky enough to have the privilege of working with Professor Kathleen Lynch in University College Dublin (UCD), who has supported this project wholeheartedly since its inception and has provided support in so many ways. I owe a huge debt of gratitude to Kathleen for all of her guidance, mentoring and support over the lifetime of this project and who has supported so many initiatives and actions over many, many years. While I was working on this research project there was an extended group of people in UCD including Mags Crean, Monica O Connor, Mariya Ivancheyva, Manolis Kalaitzake and Kathryn Keating, from whom I learned so much during chats and conversations on the fifth floor of the library building. And to the School of Education in UCD who have been very supportive to me and this project, many thanks. Jim Lawlor and Tony McCarthy have been close friends and colleagues for many years and have quietly and not so quietly supported this work since it began and have given their working lives to the struggle for the dispossessed. Thank you to all of those working in Rialto Youth Project (RYP), an organisation that I have been a part of since the 1980s and that also supported this book in so many ways. Nice one to Dannielle and to all of the staff and volunteers in the RYP. Thank you also to Rialto Community Drug Team and all who work there. Colin Coulter has provided amazing support and guidance in many different ways, from the struggles of publishing to the intricacies of the literature of class. Nice one Colin for all of the support and advice. The Irish Research Council (IRC), a number of years ago now, provided a research grant that allowed me to begin this project with some guaranteed research time. This grant made me feel that this project had some value if someone was going to invest some money in it, so big appreciation to the IRC. A big thanks to Chris Maguire, Raymond Hegarty and Tracy O Brien, who each took some amazing photographs at the beginning of this project and in many ways acted as a gateway for me. I am a member of the St Michael's Estate Regeneration Team, with whom I have worked for over 20 years in the struggle for spatial and land justice and much more besides – Rita, Eilish, Jo, Nicola, Carol, Paul, Samantha, Jim and Sasha and all who have carried the torch for the land over the years. As Rita says, La Lucha continua. I am also a member of Housing Action Now, and to all of my activist colleagues there a big thanks for listening to me talking about this project in recent years. Eilish, Nessa, Darren, Seannie, Paul, Tracy, Aengus, Trish, Lizzy, Raymond, Paula and Fiona and Feidlim and all of those involved in the Multistory project. To all in the European Action Coalition for the Right to Housing and the City, I hope you all continue the great work. I work for the Canal Communities Regional Addiction Service, without whose support this work would more than likely not have happened. They facilitated study leave and many other things that were necessary for this to get from start to finish. Pat Gates was a fantastic support to this project; and a big thanks to all of my staff colleagues: Elaine, Trish, Ciara, Norah, Paul and to Ger Doherty, who has been so supportive since coming on board as manager. To Bronagh O Neill, who also supported this work in many ways, thank you. Gemma Crowe, who did some street walking with me on occasion, a big thanks. Lynn Ruane and Rob Grant and all of the people who have participate in the Friday and Tuesday community philosophy. To all of the Community Reps on the Canal Communities Local Drug and Alcohol Task Force, Tommy, Roisin, Debbie, James, Tony, Ann and Eilish. To my late mother and father who gave so much and who knew the value of public housing, and to my sisters and brothers, I know you are always there for me Julie, Laura, Paul, Philip and Thomas and all of the extended family. To my great mates and lifelong friends Joe and Davy Boy, nice one. To Kate O Shea and everyone on the Just City project. Kate O Shea has brought new energy and ideas to the publication of this project as well as so much else. I would like to thank everyone at Policy Press for taking a risk with this book. Special thanks to Emily Watt for her persistence and dedication to this project, to Anna Richardson and Kathryn King, to Sophia Unger at Newgen Publishing, and to all of those who have worked on getting the book to print. Big thanks.

And finally, to the people of the Bridgetown Estate who gave me their time, their patience, who listened to my questions and put up with me being around the place for a while. There are some debts I will never pay. Love and best wishes. The struggle continues.

Preface

The phrase 'it's not where you live, it's how you live', was said to me on a number of occasions by different people in the Bridgetown Estate while I was doing this research project. It was usually women who used the phrase. When I first heard it, I took it as a simple desire for respect. Then I heard it a few more times and began thinking about it a bit more. It seemed to say that one can somehow get past or transcend the conditions of life that one faces and live an honourable and decent life by sheer force of will and practice. When residents used this phrase, they were usually talking about the present. How you live was referring to how you live now in the particular and the present, but it was also a more eternal or universal how you live. It is perhaps a myth, a necessary story that people tell themselves to make life bearable and to stop them from falling into the abyss. If I were to write what I thought it meant it would read something like this: *I am an honourable decent person as good as or the same as anyone else. So it doesn't matter where I live. It's how I live that really matters.* There is in the phrase a consciousness of what the big Other will say or think about me. A desire for respectability. But it is more than that. Much more. Over the course of researching and writing this book I came to understand that this question of how to live is perhaps the most fundamental of all for the people who live on the Bridgetown Estate, for the fieldwork showed clearly that this will-to-respect and the desire for a good life was confronted with harsh realities that resulted in significant struggles. The phrase brings to the surface the ontological question of the nature of being as it is made through time, but it also raises questions about unrealised possibilities of what ought to be or what could be. This dialectical tension (and enormous abyss) between past and present conditions and future possibilities is at the heart of this book.

There are good things in the present lives of public housing tenants. There are practices of love and care, of nurturing, sharing and solidarity. There is also the odd belly laugh here and there. Without being sentimental, these are sometimes almost all that people have. In Bridgetown, people could not survive without each other. They cannot live individualistic lives just for themselves because they depend too much on each other and need each other too much. Given that we are relational beings, this is a positive relationality of care and support. But there are also bad things and sources of suffering. These are negative relationalities when life is strictly conditioned by lack and scarcity and by violence, anguish and shame, with little distance from necessity as people work out how they will get from day to day and week to week. Contrary to the utilitarian view that hunger is good sauce, poverty is not ennobling and provides fertile soil for misery, alienation and violence. The question therefore of causes and how problems get framed and explained is very important. The research chapters of the book will prove that the class and gender structures have a significant bearing on how one lives in a public housing estate and, by extension, beyond. Class is both *inherently material* and *morally significant*. It is not a case of 'either/or' but one of 'both/and'. Class has an address in that it is located somewhere in space-time, in that lives are lived out and end in particular places. This is the geography of class, and it grids and striates the city and country with clear lines of demarcation. We live here and you live there. We live like this, you live like that. If the how is important, so too is the where. The factory floor or work site was decreed in the past and present as perhaps the fundamental site of class struggle. This work invites the reader to extend the notion of class and gender struggle into the everyday lives of public housing tenants. For struggle they do against various forms of power, lack, scarcity, exploitation, violence and neglect. We must therefore see public housing estates as critical components in the reproduction of the class and gender structures against analyses that posit them as essentialised places of 'deprivation' and 'disadvantage'. They are one of the hearts of inequality on the sleeve of modern Ireland. Admission criteria determine that only those in the lower reaches of the class structure are eligible, making them relatively homogeneous and unique locations. And while this was done to ensure access to housing for those with least means, the result is the production of particular class forms. Public housing estates are, like Traveller halting sites, the ghetto, the banlieu and the barrio, visible collective manifestations of inequality. And yet, a mixture of political ideology and deliberate amnesia often render them either invisible or as pathological spaces. This relationship between class and place, or to put it in phenomenological terms this symbiosis between matter and consciousness, will be important throughout. There is also a view that neglects place and space, and that argues that only people have consciousness, implying that streets and buildings are inert and immobile, so why do they matter? But, alongside material conditions, buildings, streets, hallways, balconies, open spaces, these inanimate *things*, as it were, define the existence of Bridgetown residents. They limit and constrain, but they also enable one to learn and to become a social being. Residents accustom themselves to place. They resist it too. The Bridgetown Estate has a being all of its own. It contains presence and absence and burrows deep into the psyche of those who live there. Lives happen here in this place. Stories carry the past into the present for a future yet to be. The relationship between the physical-practical-social-economic-historical-affective world one inhabits and how one lives is crucial. This begs the question: could things be different? And, if so, what role has research to play in this? I agree with those who use a critical social science approach, and take the view that research has an important role to play in removing the sources and causes of such suffering. This is its axiological function. This study is of an urban public housing estate in the city of Dublin, Ireland.

This research explores the lives of the tenants of that public housing estate and was undertaken in order to try to get a deeper understanding of their lives and to try to help change them for the better.

Postscript

It is a sunny day in May 2020, around noon. Myself, Rosy and Charlie are talking about the current state of the COVID-19 lockdown. They tell me that they have both been playing the outdoor bingo the previous evening. "It's all done with the social distancing and it's a fiver a book," Rosy says. Neither of them won anything, they tell me. I share some sweets that I have in my pocket and, after looking at my latex gloves, Rosy says to me, "I knew you wouldn't want them sweets back." Charlie has been over, helping get food ready for the older people who will have their meals dropped at their doors. As we are there, Nadia comes out of one of the new blocks. Even though she had said she would never surrender her old flat until she was given another ground-floor flat, she is now in a first-floor unit and is using the lift she said she would never use. She has had an operation on her knee, but her foot remains twisted. "I'm hopin to get that done soon," she says, pointing at her foot. Even so, she has a tartan box trolley and is taking a bus to the nearest shopping centre. Young men are coming and going in the background, heads self-shaved. We walk out of the estate to the main road. Nadia says to me "I wouldn't go that local shop there, not with what they charge you. That's why I am getting the bus to the shopping centre." She crosses the busy road slowly with her trolley and I promise to visit her new flat soon. Rosy says that she has been off the drink for a while but has had a little bit of a wobble because of the lockdown. When we get to the local shop she says "No, we are going to the other one, the gargle is cheaper there. It's three euro instead of three fifty a can." There are more people on the streets than there have been recently, Charlie says, and more cars as well. We meet other residents of the estate on the way back as we pass the barber's, which is closed. When we get back to the block we chat for a little while in the sunshine and I say "Good luck".

1

Introduction

Being is never me alone, it is always me and those like me. (Georges Bataille, *Oeuvres. Completes* 8:297, quoted in Jean Luc Nancy, 1991, p 33)

Given that they are on the one hand so prominent while on the other almost invisible, it may seem strange to ask: what sort of a thing or object, then, is a public housing estate? How and by what is it constituted? My conclusion from this work is that public housing estates are not just the locations of but are constituted and utterly defined by class and gender relations and processes. This may seem obvious, but I want to argue, especially in the latter half of the book, that public housing estates are social forms that embody and reflect the stratified, differentiated and realist nature of the societies we live in. They are 'real' objects that contain within themselves the sediment and (continually changing and moving) geology of class (Savage, 2015) and gender structures. Trying to describe, analyse and specify the significance of such relations, mechanisms and processes is the focus of this book. This is therefore an attempt to engage dialogically with the object that is a public housing estate in order to maximise explanatory power and to make 'the analysis as precise, but only as precise as the nature of the subject permits' (Bhaskar 2009, p 168). The reason why this is important is because such mechanisms and the processes they entail are, more often than not, unperceivable, and are visible only in their effects. I will argue, therefore, that as well as understanding what we perceive there is also a need for causal criteria for understanding the ongoing reproduction of public housing estates. Sayer (2000, p 149) underlines the nature of this problem when he says that 'Grasping the whole is more difficult than grasping what happens next in the story.' The whole, as it were, and such effects, are what characterise the Bridgetown Estate and are evident in the ethnographic chapters that follow. The people who live here are labourers, care workers, retail workers, hospital workers, factory workers, truck drivers, make-up artists, taxi drivers, bricklayers, carpenters, plasterers, employees of multinational companies, state employees, shop workers, community workers, community employment workers. They are also quite often 'the unemployed'. They therefore occupy particular positions within the social system. They also are at the same time friends, lovers, partners, kin, mothers, fathers, brothers, sisters, sons, daughters, grandparents, uncles, aunts, nephews, nieces and cousins. To live, they must necessarily engage in a range of social relations. All have pasts, presents and futures. Time envelops them from birth to death. A public housing estate is therefore a micro-totality or world that is tied or knotted to a macro-totality where these economic and non-economic processes mutually condition and reinforce each other and make life particularly what it is. The Bridgetown Estate is therefore a 'concentration of many determinations', and manifests within itself 'the unity of diverse' to use Marx's (1993, p 101) phrase from the *Grundrisse*. Or, as Hegel writes in the *Phenomenology* (1977, p 380) 'an object of perception in general is a thing of many properties'. Life on the estate is therefore 'overdetermined' or multiply determined (Resnick and Wolff, 1987) by these mutually constitutive class and non-class processes and mechanisms that contain innate contradictions, and that are ceaselessly if unnoticeably changing through time. They contain the perceivable and the unperceivable, but are nevertheless underpinned by systematic mechanisms of cause and effect. The Bridgetown Estate is a congealed conjuncture and condensation of such effects and such generative mechanisms. It is a 'process in product in process' in that it is, has been and will be in various states of change, becoming and negation (Bhaskar, 2008b, p 220). It is not now what it was at the beginning. In this book, I am going to try to analyse and peel back the most important of these determinations and analyse how they mutually condition and produce life on the estate. I would like to think that there is something new in this 'realist' presentation of a public housing estate, and that there is a logic of social scientific discovery present in this work.

As part of this exploration, I will focus on the nature of life on the Bridgetown Estate and try to understand, to explain why it is the way it is and ask, could it be different, as in, could people live better lives? Could we live in societies where the life-destroying effects of class, gender or race had no impact or left no trace on how we live? Is emancipation possible; or perhaps, more to the point, necessary? My answer to this question is a simple 'yes'. There are undoubtedly authentic or good parts to the lives of Bridgetown residents, but there is also the inauthentic and the oppressive rooted in the class and gender processes mentioned earlier. As we shall see, life on the Bridgetown Estate is conditioned by scarcity and lack, but this does not *have* to be the case. It could be otherwise. Conditions divide people from themselves. I believe and want to argue that there is a 'wrong' (Ranciere, 1999, pp 21–42), that is, an injustice, at the heart of life on the Bridgetown Estate, and this originates in the mechanisms that define the existing social-political-economic-affective order. Central to this is the idea that the people who live on the Bridgetown Estate are involved in struggles over how to live. At a basic material level this fundamentally means how to live with meagre resources based on class position and location, but it also no less means struggles over the how to live of emotion and love and nourishing and sustaining each other. Residents are involved in struggles over valued and dignified ways of life. The logic or relationality therefore that governs life on the Bridgetown Estate is a fundamentally material-affective logic rather than one that is instrumental-strategic; one that demands that residents must survive and care for each other. Practices are determined by struggles over such goods in and of themselves as opposed to the advantages they bring vis-à-vis other groups, as in the case of making distinction or difference a priority. Necessity and care are perhaps life's guiding principles. Writing about the nature of practices and their relationship to the 'virtues' McIntyre (2007), makes a distinction between the 'internal and external goods' of a practice. Internal goods are immanent to a practice itself and involve the innate satisfaction that one gets from doing a practice such as childrearing or playing games or playing music, while external goods have to do with the external rewards of things like money, prestige or the fame that practices may bring. By necessity, the focus of practices in the Bridgetown Estate revolves almost entirely around the internal goods of practices. The scope for attaining significant external goods is generally minimal. Lives are oriented toward use values and practices are based on securing the necessities of life and the internal goods that practices embedded in relations such as loving and caring bring. The difficulty is that residents produce and reproduce their worlds and engage in such struggles, and this is the important bit: they do this under conditions for the most part *not* of their own choosing. Practices are therefore conditioned and inflected by critically important things such as (lack of) access to various forms of resources and forms of capital (Bourdieu, 1986; Bourdieu and Wacquant, 1992).

In other words, Bridgetown residents, while living subjective lives, are occupants of objective class positions in relation with other classes in the class structure. They undoubtedly possess many different abilities, capacities and competencies, perhaps not least of which are the skills of survival. They possess many tendencies and powers that remain unexercised because neither the opportunities nor the resources are available for the exercise of such powers. Unlike the middle-class, their lives are not characterised by the possession of property, nor do they hold positions of bureaucratic or organisational power, nor do they occupy dominant positions in the field of culture. Or, to put it in more simple, question form, what does one own? What work does one do either paid or/and unpaid? What credentials does one possess or what sort of leisure does one have or take part in? What sort of care does one receive (Savage et al, 1992; Olin Wright, 1997; Mau, 2015; Lynch, 2022)? It is improbable, to say the least, that they will inherit property or privilege or collectively break the class ceiling (Friedman and Laurison, 2020) to become affluent or rich. Nor, for instance, for all of the time working on this research project, did I meet anyone who lives on the estate who was paid to think or to write or to make art for a living. One generally needs freedom from necessity (see Bourdieu, 1993; Lynch et al, 2009, p 17) to be able to do such things. And yet, residents' thought and being is thoroughly engaged in constant creative dialogue with material conditions and day-to-day living. Bridgetown residents, therefore, operate within tightly controlled and disciplined work (and other) environments and are located within subordinate positions and places within class and gender relations. They are much more likely to take and be given orders than to give them, as we shall see. Choices and options are strictly conditioned and circumscribed, therefore, by the lack of material and immaterial resources. These mechanisms place significant limitations on them in relation to what is and isn't possible. The great problem with such structures and the point that will be made here is that they prohibit people like those of the Bridgetown Estate and countless others from finding and living out their true or essential nature(s). Or, to put it another way, life would be (far) better if the systems and regimes of exploitation, domination and injustice that underpin such structures and keep them in place were removed. How this will or could happen is an important question and raises important social-scientific questions about the relationship between facts and values, and between theory and practices (Bhaskar, 2015, p 54). And while struggles would undoubtedly remain, the possibility for flourishing would be greatly enhanced upon the removal of such structures and mechanisms of domination. Questions of justice, therefore, are centrally connected to the lives of those who live in public housing estates and to geography more generally (Fanstein, 1996; Merryfield and Swyngedouw, 1996; Harvey, 2009).

The conditions on the Bridgetown Estate are therefore not the product of inherent pathology, nor do they arise from of a 'culture of poverty' as McKenzie (2015) has eloquently and correctly argued. It is incorrect and perhaps all too easy to describe such estates under such rhyming rubrics as 'poor people, poor places', as estates in Limerick were described by Pringle et al (1999), as if one was necessarily the causal factor of the other and they were somehow naturally symbiotic and auto-generative. Instead, we need to discover and outline how such conditions are causally produced by particular mechanisms and sets of essential relations that place and situate residents in particular positions. The contingent and changing nature of such mechanisms has had significant effects on life on the estate over time and reflects the fact that class and class relations are dynamic, historical processes that change form and function over time (Archer et al, 1998, p 39). But this does not lessen their effects, for all that. The challenge therefore is to show that public housing estates are the product and outcome of sets of necessary relations that are grounded in structures such as those of the economic, the affective and the spatio-temporal. Marx's statement that 'All science would be superfluous if the outward appearances and essences of things directly coincided' expresses the importance of going beyond what our senses tell us (Marx quoted in Bhaskar, 2015, p 8). In much of Irish social policy until now public housing estates in Ireland have been largely theorised through the lens of deprivation and disadvantage and are presented and explained as atomised, non-relational, singular entities that are immanent to themselves and in which everyday life and conditions somehow are autonomously or internally (re)produced within estates, as it were. Theories and discourses of deprivation, disadvantage and social inclusion have been hugely influential in (re)presenting and promoting this sort of atomistic ontology as a 'true' or 'essentialist' version of reality. A spatialised and largely positivist topology of deprivation has developed from such discourses that fragments and compartmentalises and misses or perhaps even deliberately ignores the necessary relations that govern lives and configure them in very particular ways. From a deprivation–disadvantage, perspective estates and areas within cities and the country at large are colour coded, with scores given according to deprivation indexes and rankings. 'Measures' of deprivation magically appear in stacks and piles distributed randomly across the country, waiting to be discovered once one inputs the requisite 'variables' into a processor. A colour-coded map tells how 'disadvantaged' or how 'affluent' an area or neighbourhood is. In this schema, individualised variables define one's life, and not social relations between groups. Notions of deprivation and disadvantage have become one, if not the dominant, mode of interpreting and explaining the lives of public housing tenants. (The same concepts also play a key role in funding relationships that demand docility and obedience and general acceptance of the deprivation thesis (see Kelleher and O Neill, 2018). And while there is often recognition of the importance of the spatial in such approaches, it is my view that this approach mystifies and depoliticises both object and subject, as it were, using what is effectively a positivist-empiricist approach to spatiality that sees and presents only unrelated variables and has little or nothing to say on necessary relations or class or gender processes. Things are only what they are on the surface and, as Soja (1985, pp 99, 100) has pointed out, this approach creates the 'illusion of transparency', as if all that exists is what we see (variables, inputs and so on) in front of us (Pringle et al, 1999; Moran, 2006; Bhaskar, 2009, pp 282–285; Hourigan, 2011).

The two edited sister volumes on Social Housing in Ireland (Fahey, 1999; Norris, 2014) are important in this regard in that, on one hand, they highlight the value of public/social housing over many decades in Ireland. And yet, on the other hand and more importantly, they detach the people who live in public housing estates and the estates themselves from the larger social reality in which they are embedded, thus generally ignoring necessary or intrinsic relations and placing the emphasis instead on concepts such as disadvantage, deprivation and other concepts such as that of 'neighbourhood liveability' that presuppose essentialised and internalised perspectives of public housing tenants and the estates they live in. Such analyses, in my view, reify people and places and are anti-relational and contrary to the relational (Bourdieu and

Wacquant, 1992; Bhaskar, 2015, pp 25–79) approach taken here. In chapters such as 'Changing Disadvantage in Social Housing' (Haase in Norris, 2014, p 23), which 'examines social change and disadvantage', the fate of the people in the seven public housing estates under study is tied, it seems, to the ebb and flow of an arbitrary and anonymous economic tide. Indicators of social class position are included as designators, but there is little or nothing to explain causal mechanisms or dynamic processes as to how and why things have come to be this way. Class is objectified in scales (Olin Wright, 1997, p 34) and de-relationalised. It becomes solely a gradational category and not a relational one. Time and history also tend to be reified and class positions exist without class relations in the deprivation–disadvantage schema. We have vertical disconnected stacks instead of the real matrix of social-relational ligatures. Places and communities are (falsely) enclosed and separated from each other and from the city and beyond. They become immanent and absolute to themselves. There is scant understanding as to how lives are constituted by the many economic and political processes that make up the social totality. The same is true for gender positions and structures. There is a gap here between the 'words used and the things described' (Ranciere, 1999, p 85), in that they do not correspond. Neither is there any real sense of how people got to where they are, in that they are presented as beings largely without histories or practices or traditions, as it were. They are literally 'beings without relation' (Luc Nancy, 1991, p 4). One is left with the impression from such studies that estates and the people in them live detached lives cut off from class or gender relations and the life of the city itself or beyond, and who are also largely devoid of emotion or passion as to what happens to themselves, their families or to those around them.

What passes for knowledge of public housing tenants and the working class in general, then, is therefore very important, for there is a strong possibility (that undoubtedly exists here as well, and of which others can judge) of more of the colonisation of working class lives by academics and others, especially in the media, who are in privileged positions to write and provide 'definitive' accounts of the working class and who can often appear to know more about the working class than they know about themselves (Pierse, 2011). There are precedents for such colonisation as it relates to academic research in the field of education in Ireland as described by Lynch and O Neill (1994). Or, as Lefebvre (1991, p 10) puts it in a slightly different way, there is a difference 'between a knowledge which serves power and a form of knowing which refuses to acknowledge power'. On the same theme Resnick and Wolff (1987, p 34) argue that 'the predominant epistemology and the predominant class process provide conditions for each other's existence'. The production of 'knowledge' is therefore not neutral, in that those with power and various forms of capital therefore quite often get to tell their story or the story they want to tell about others, often with visceral effects. This is often done under the guise of an objective, value-free social science. The myth of the neutrality of social science proposed by Weber is far reaching and long lasting (Gouldner, 1962) and often functions to conceal particular worldviews and positions, quite often those of the dominant. This is ideology working at its most effective when social reality is taken for granted or as 'natural' (Elster, 1982, pp 123–148; Zizek, 1989; Bhaskar, 2015 pp 69–70). The people who live in public housing estates do not merely occupy hypostatised frozen positions, then, they are and have been enmeshed as a class in prolonged and intense sets of social relations that define the nature of their lives to a large extent. How their lives are framed and explained has very important implications and results. What stories are told about them and by whom is very important. With some notable (biographical and fictional) exceptions (for some see Hoggart, 1957; Steedman, 1987; Pierse, 2011; Ranciere, 2012; Parkinson, 2016; Louis, 2017; Ruane, 2018; Emecheta, 2018; McGarvey, 2018) the working-class are often more written about than writing about themselves. They can become mere ragdolls for research that are dissected and then badly resewn. The power, effect and political rationale behind ideological, hostile and antagonistic representations of the working-class has been well documented (Adair, 2002; Skeggs, 2002, 2004; Tyler, 2008; Jones, 2012; McKenzie, 2015).

Against such atomistic ontologies, therefore, I will argue for a social ontology that places the people of the Bridgetown Estate four-square enmeshed within sets of relations both within and without the estate, and therefore work from a relational conception of social life and social reality within which the lives of residents are shaped by the struggles between groups in a society over its material, cultural, spatial and affective resources and 'goods' in the broad sense. This remains the case even if such struggles are not overtly conscious or political. The 'attractiveness of a neighbourhood' (Norris, 2014, p 2) is undoubtedly important, but what of lifelong struggles for goods in a deeper sense of finding valued ways to live, to find and do interesting work, to love and care for children or to put food on the table every day? Material conditions and neighbourhood life are not independent of each other, for both are causally related. What is happening in my immediate neighbourhood is important, but what of the dynamics and causal relations and powers inherent in the changing social relations of (post-)industrial capitalism, or patriarchy for that matter, on the people who live in public housing estates? Just because they are not visible or are difficult to decipher does not mean that they do not exist or have significant and lasting effects. They do. Writing about the difference between good and bad abstractions, Sayer (1998, p 127) highlights the importance of distinguishing between necessary and non-necessary relations or, to put the same thing differently, between internal and external relations:

Good or 'rational' abstractions should isolate necessary relationships. The concrete, as a unity of diverse determinations, is a combination of several necessary relationships but the form of the combination is contingent, and therefore only determinable through empirical research … the same point can be made by using a distinction between external and internal relations. The relation between a person and a lump of earth is external and contingent in the sense that each object can exist without the other. On the other hand relations between landlord and tenant, master and slave are internal and necessary in that each part of the relation depends upon its relation to the other. … Theories make their strongest claims about the abstract level, about necessary and internal relations, about causal powers which exist in virtue of the nature of particular things.

This book will therefore engage with this social–ontological problematic of *how to live* on the basis that such 'necessary and internal relations' of interdependency shape and determine how people live on the Bridgetown Estate. Imbued within phrases used by residents, what Sperber (1982, pp 166–171) calls 'semi propositions', such as *It's not where you live, it's how you live*, and *What goes around comes around*, are deep structural and cultural contradictions about the nature of being and how and why it is or has come to be that way and the relations that determine it or could possibly change it. How does such being come to be? How is it this sort of being and not another? Why do residents spend their days doing unpaid work, searching for or waiting for food or looking for paid work or cleaning or trying to negotiate better housing through the city council? Or, to put it slightly differently, why do these particular conditions exist in this particular place at this particular time? To borrow an example from Bhaskar (2015, p 28), if the writing of a cheque presupposes a banking system or the existence of a tribeswoman/man presupposes a tribal society, what must be necessary for the existence of a public housing estate? A public housing system, yes; but perhaps more importantly, a particular form of society, one defined and made up of and structured by fundamental and subsumed class processes (Resnick and Wolff, 1987, p 122). Public housing estates are the product and outcome of a society and global economic capitalist system that sifts and segregates according to tight principles of class and gender relations. Like Grenfell Tower, the Bridgetown Estate is therefore a physical and visible manifestation of class structures and class relations in Ireland, but for the most part the significance of this goes unnoticed and improperly analysed, which sustains relations of domination and inequality that are very much in place. Writing about the 'poverty propaganda' that smears people in public housing as work-shy or lazy, Tracy Shildrick says of the people who lived in the Grenfell Tower:

Perhaps unsurprisingly and in contrast to the popular and political stigmatisation of places like Grenfell, *the tower housed the working class.* People who were all too often working and who resided in one of the richest cities in the world, and who were linked by a state that failed them in the cruellest way possible. (Shildrick, 2018, pp 14–15, emphasis added)

To connect this to the nature of being on the Bridgetown Estate, then, there is the current nature or way life 'is', that carries the sediment of the past transmitted within it and that is continually mutating in important ways, most often unnoticeably through time. The 'is' is problematic within itself, for it presupposes something that could always be other or different. This raises the related normative question of how life 'ought to be' or could be, which invokes the possibility of what Aristotle (2004) in the *Nichomachean Ethics* calls *eudamonia*, that is, the possibility of happiness or a 'good life' and what it would mean to flourish. McIntyre (2007, p 52) describes this problematic as the difference between 'man-as-he-happens-to-be and man-as-he-could-be-if-he-realised-his-essential-nature'. He proposes that 'Ethics is the science which is to enable men to understand how to make the transition from the former to the latter.' (In my view this applies to everyone – that is, not just men). This gap, as it were, has been described by Ranciere (1999) in a different way when he says 'The wrong instituted by politics is not primarily class warfare; it is the difference of each class from itself.' In Ranciere's thought, this difference and 'wrong' constitutes the 'disagreement' at the core of politics as we know it and is that which separates how we live now from how we ought to live or could live (Ranciere, 1999, pp 18–19). This shift, then, from is to ought, from facts to values, from theory to practice, which has a particular history in social and philosophical thought, is central to the philosophy and programme of critical social science. The long list and broad church of those practising critical social science and philosophy argue that we should be critical of practices that are damaging to people or cause them suffering and work for the removal of such practices and their causes. Such practices include exploitation, racism, inequality, carelessness, ableism, transphobism and violence, to name but some. There are important distinctions to be made between subjective, objective and systemic violence, for quite often commentators and analysts of public housing focus solely on the prurient of subjective violence while negating the effects of objective or systemic violence that is often procedural and full of neglect (Bourdieu, 1991, pp 163–70; Wacquant, 2009; Zizek, 2009; Eagleton, 2010). *All* of such forms feed through the Bridgetown Estate. I am therefore in agreement with the emancipatory impulse of critical social science (Fay, 1987; Sayer, 2000) that says we should be critical of practices that cause harm or suffering, and I also agree fully that research has a role to play in removing such practices, and here I am going to apply it to the foregoing ethnography of the Bridgetown Estate. Such an approach has also been called 'explanatory critique' (Bhaskar, 2015), or 'a critique of everyday life' (Lefebvre, 2014). So, if constituting well or properly the object of a public housing estate is the first challenge, the critique of harmful practices and their replacement with those that promote human flourishing is as important, if not more so.

A note on research methodology

This research project began in 2014 as the Bridgetown Estate began a process of physical and social change. I began to make contact with people on the estate, some of whom I knew from previous work on public housing estates over many years of community work in the city of Dublin. I had a vague idea and urge in my head that it could or would be useful to chronicle the lives of the residents of a public housing estate. I felt that there was a real need to try to get a better and deeper grasp of the story of the public housing estate. I also felt and still feel that there is relatively little written on the Irish public housing estate(s) comparable to studies in Britain or in Europe or the US, especially those undertaken using participant observation and fieldwork. Part of my motivation had to do with the way that so many estates and a significant part of the working-class culture of the city in this particular form was fragmenting and disappearing from the surface of the city and, if nothing else, to try to put something on the record for posterity. I had become frustrated with the general narrative that I often found myself speaking, or speaking through me, and with my desire to escape the very pervasive doxa of the deprivation–disadvantage paradigm. My major aim was to try to eventually write something that got at the difficulties and struggles residents faced, while also trying to hear and to understand what was good about life on an estate such as this. Motive and method are undoubtedly different, but they are also connected, in that I thought the best way to answer these questions was by way of using an ethnographic approach of participant observation and conversation. Photography was an early entry into this process of change, taking images of people and of the interior and exterior spaces of the estate. A small group of excellent photographers helped out at this stage. People were beginning to move from flats into other flats, or off the estate altogether. I applied for and was successful in being awarded a research grant from the Irish Research Council in 2016 and this helped the work to develop and grow and for me to spend some part of the week working in University College Dublin with Professor Kathleen Lynch. I carried out thirty hour-long recorded conversations with residents of the Bridgetown Estate. The age range of residents varied from young adults in their early twenties to people in their sixties. I was continuing to build relationships with various people on the estate while carrying out the recorded conversations, thinking all the while about the difference between what people say and what they do and the tension and the gaps between the saying and the doing. I have kept contact with people from these recorded conversations, checking in and hearing how things have changed or not changed much. There were some people who didn't want to participate in a recorded conversation but were more than generous in sharing their lives with me over many hours of conversation. Over the course of wandering in and out of the estate and talking to and making contact with people, I began to spend more time with one particular group of people. I was nervous that they wouldn't accept me at first, but they did. This contact became more regular and intense between 2016 and 2019. I would hang around with them in the estate in various locations, a lot of time on the steps outside individual flats. I would walk the streets with them. I would sit inside flats as life passed and the mundane and the extraordinary were discussed. I would go wherever they were going and meet whoever they were meeting. To the supermarkets, the hairdresser's, the off-licence, the religious house, community projects, local shops, I went. There were bus trips to Knock, the religious shrine in the west of Ireland, bus trips to the zoo, bus and walking trips in and out of the city. Lots of walking and talking and listening and asking stupid questions of people. I wrote and typed hundreds of thousands of words of field-notes over this period. In 2019–20 I spent a substantial period of time analysing all of the gathered and collected material, looking for themes and patterns and causal connections. The chapters of the book are a result of this recording and analysis and the conclusion is a first tentative attempt at making sense of how class, gender and place structure the lives of public housing tenants. I officially stopped doing last pieces of fieldwork, checking with people, in the middle of 2020 as COVID-19 was taking hold and lockdowns were coming into being, but I have continued to stay in touch with many people from the estate right up to the present time in 2022 as the book goes to publication.

Outline of the book

The rest of the book is structured in the following way. Chapter 2 is the first of the ethnographic chapters and describes a place in flux as the estate undergoes a process of physical and social change and transformation. Chapters 3 and 4 'Work Ethic 1' and 'Work Ethic 2' are based on observations and recorded interviews primarily with two men and two women from the estate about their working lives, paid and unpaid, and their long-term relation to the estate. Chapters 5 to 9 are based on my participation for an extended period of time over almost three years with a group of residents of the estate as they try to live from day to day, going about their daily lives. These chapters explore different aspects of the lives of residents, from sourcing food, to struggles with money, to the issue of disability, to the use and importance of words and stories in their lives. Part II of the book, Chapters 10–13, tries to place the fieldwork and observations within a critical-realist framework for understanding a public housing estate. It builds a bridge between the manifest phenomena described in the ethnographic chapters and the structures of class, gender and space that play such a crucial role in shaping and moulding residents' lives. The importance and significance of class is the subject of Chapter 11. My argument is that class relations and class processes provide a much more coherent explanation and understanding of public housing than does the deprivation–disadvantage schema. Chapter 12 deals with the affective domain, and particularly with the gendered nature of life on the estate and relations of love and care and dependency and interdependency. The focus in this chapter is on the particular struggles of women. Chapter 13 brings the reader back to the place that is the Bridgetown Estate and analyses the relationship between place and space and the relationship between the perceived, the conceived and the lived aspects of the Bridgetown Estate.

PART I

Ethnography

2

Should I stay or should I go?

'If the steps could talk they'd have some stories to tell.' (Maxine)

I am sitting outside Maxine's flat one day. As we are sitting, a heavyset, perspiring city council maintenance man emerges and tells her that "you can have any coloured tiles you like as long as they are white". He chuckles at his own joke as he goes about the work of replacing some of the tiles above the sink in the kitchen. His one-liner seems a good place to start, in that the council worker, albeit unwittingly, says something profound about Maxine's subordinate position not just within the Irish public housing system but perhaps, more importantly, within the class and gender structures that play such a significant role in shaping and determining the lives that she and other Bridgetown residents lead. The illusion of choice and free will collides against the real of the boundaries and limitations that circumscribe a life. These structures are tight and reproduce themselves over generations, and are critical sources of suffering.

The year is 2014 and the Bridgetown Estate is in a state of flux. Block A and most of Block B in the Bridgetown Estate are being de-tenanted in order that these same de-tenanted blocks may be demolished and rebuilt or, in some cases, the old shells will be kept and retrofitted. Everyone in these two blocks must move now to one of a limited number of available empty flats within the estate, but the far greater proportion must move off site. This chapter focuses on an estate as it changes from what it was and is into something else, and how residents engage with this change and what they must do practically. Some residents state clearly that they want to move back as soon as the blocks are redone, while others wish to leave and never come back. Some will decide whether to stay permanently in their 'transition' accommodation, even though they have a 'golden letter' (as residents call them) that gives them a right to return when the blocks have been rebuilt. This 'golden letter' is subject to specific conditions on having no rent arrears and no anti-social behaviour violations and may possibly be revoked if these conditions are breached. This is the first phase of a long-term project for the entire estate that is to be done in four or five phases over a number of years.

The blocks, balconies, flats, hallways, steps and open spaces are the parts that make up the whole of the Bridgetown Public Housing Estate. The muscular forms of the blocks were set down in rows with sharp, angular precision, with large garden spaces uniformly separating one from the next. The estate is all straight sight lines, flint-edged right angles and symmetrical geometry and is more Corbusier than Gaudi. The architectonics of the blocks are important, for they have shaped the way people have lived and interacted for many decades, even if this is about to change. Each of the blocks is a self-contained amphitheatre of sorts. Life is played out between the backstage privacy of one's flat and the frontstage commons that is the open space of a block. The membrane that separates backstage from frontstage can be thin and porous, with people coming and going. In this public space there is a sense of lives lived and shared in common for an omnipotent audience. Levels of interaction and sociability are high. Contemporarily in much public discourse such design is usually described in purely negative terms, in that the nature and form of such open space is determined to have played a causal role in the rise of 'anti-social behaviour' and drug dealing within estates. The resolution of such issues has seen a rush to enclose space. And yet, the original design also allows supreme ease of access and contact between people, and there are few barriers to prohibit movement or contact within the public realm of a block save one's front door. The blocks are agoric spaces of free association. On exiting a flat or entering a block there is the possibility and likelihood of any number of interpersonal interactions, traversing age and gender. The blocks work as a sort of inverted Panopticon, in that instead of one supreme gaze overseeing every individual, gaze and perception are shared between all of the flats in a block, in that every flat has a visual–aural–oral connection with almost all others. The one and the many play and feed off each other. When a resident opens a front door there is a visual and verbal reciprocity in that they can see and converse with almost everyone, and everyone can do so with them. Residents will often call or 'shout up' to neighbours, inviting them down into a block or into a flat for a chat. Waves of sound rise and fall. One moment nothing, and the next a cacophony of voices echo and reverberate throughout the acoustic space. "What's the story? What are you up to? It's poxy out today isn't it?" Such openness will change, as new designs for the estate will push for more enclosed, socially insulated living forms.

When one crosses the threshold into a block it is the steps and open hallways that function as natural points of congregation and interaction. Almost every ground-floor flat in the Bridgetown Estate has a raised step at its front door. The buildings were raised because of the water table and the small lakes of fetid water that lie beneath. Here is a sort of subterranean subconscious where only rats dwell. Damp has been a problem in the estate for many years. The steps provide a natural seating area. There is a sort of inverse relationship between flat size and step space, with smaller flats having the larger step space. The steps are a peculiarity of design and have been put to use by many residents as an extension of their living space out into the immediate surrounds of their flat. They act as natural aprons of sorts, and while some are or become highly active, others are only rarely used. The steps function as impromptu gathering spaces for sociality and for important rituals such as talking and chatting, the taking of tea, coffee, a smoke or, less often, the drinking of alcohol. The practice of 'sitting out' on the steps that residents often mention has a seasonality to it and takes place with special intensity in summer, when people primitively follow the Earth's rotation from one side of a block to the other, chasing the last of the sun's rays. The steps are places where young people talk and children play and where new-born babies are brought to be shown off for the first time in newly gifted clothes adorned with the baby's name. In the past they were often the locations for intense and volatile card games, but not so much now. On one occasion as I sat with Maxine at her step a young man from the block turned up riding his horse, and the day after this at an adjacent step a lengthy discussion took place between a local resident, myself and two men from the Legion of Mary going round the estate preaching salvation. On another day in Block B, I was told the story of Eddie who had recently passed away but was renowned for his ability and dexterity to fix any problem with Sellotape. 'Bring it up to Eddie, he'll sort it.' Even in a digital age, the steps and hallways remain active spaces of sociability where profane daily life is lived out and mulled over. They remain important nodes in the estate's information network.

It is at the steps where this ethnography begins, as I make contact with a whole circle of people that populate a block and who congregate and chat about daily life, and also about whether they are moving temporarily while the rebuilding is done or leaving permanently, never to come back. They are invested and passionate about what will happen to them. It is around the steps and hallways where residents discuss intensely who is staying and who is going, whether people want to stay in the estate or leave and not come back, where people want to go, who is leaving when, what they want from the 'moves' and how they are fairing out, asking each other "Did you get sorted?" Residents discuss the machinations of the public housing field that presents itself to them through terms such as 'the list', 'transfers', 'priority', 'transition', 'moves' and, more recently, the increasing significance for tenants of penalties for 'rent arrears' and 'antisocial behaviour'. People tell me that there is a new form called a 'Section 15' that deals specifically with 'antisocial'. There is also the one great upside that is only occasionally mentioned, but implicitly understood: the affordability of the rent. Maxine's rent is €37 a week for a one-bedroom flat. I know this because she shouts it to a neighbour one day as she crosses the block. The public housing field that they find themselves enmeshed in works through a set of very particular rules and conditions. At this point in time, residents find themselves within an estate that is in motion, as it were, and that is tied into and conditioned by the rules of the public housing system.

There are a number of steps in Block A that act as social orbits, and one of those is the one outside Maxine's flat, which is next to the old and now unused rubbish chute and an open hallway where one ascends to the balconies above. There are communal bins now, in the middle of the block. Balconies overhang the steps, giving them a degree of shelter from the rain. Groups of people often form and gather around the step and the hall to have a smoke and a chat or a cup of tea and a biscuit or to participate, like characters from Beckett's prose, in any of a multiple possible series of these. The step and the surrounding vicinity draws into its magnetic field a range of people, some of whom live in close proximity around and above Maxine's flat and some from other parts of the estate. A myriad of social and personal relationships feed in and out of this junction box, some fleeting and momentary, some deep and profound. Maxine has lived in the Bridgetown Estate all of her life, first as a child with her own parents and siblings and then as a single parent with her own children, as a tenant in her own right. Since her mother left the estate some years ago, Maxine's flat has become a de facto family home where some of her brothers come to visit on an almost daily basis. The visits are reflective of patterns of wider descent and family lines that have long flowed beyond the estate, but that draw people back time and again. Her brother Tony, who now lives in state-supported private rented accommodation, visits her almost daily. He has his own connections and friendships here but, as he says himself, a lot of his friends are dead that he grew up with. When he talks about the fact that his sister will soon leave the estate, he says that it won't be a problem and he will just get on with things, but upon reflection he says, "actually it will be strange after all the years here, these were great flats to grow up in as a kid and we had great times, they were great times until all of that stuff happened [he doesn't get into it], so yeah, it will be funny not comin here". He has been doing a training course in welding and explains the nuances of Mig and Tig welding to me, but he has had great difficulty obtaining any sort of paid work for many years. There is another man, Jack, a friend of Tony's, whom I encounter almost daily and who, like Tony, leads a similar daily migratory existence, leaving a hostel in the early morning and spending his days in the estate and returning to the hostel at night time, before the 10 pm curfew. Jack also has strong family connections in the estate and both of them demonstrate the pull the estate has for them and their will and need to return day after day. They know each other well, and both of them always offer warm welcomes when I come into the block. They tell me stories of being in prison at the same time but not meeting each other. Jack says that he didn't go to 'normal' school but was sent away to '—' and says of it, "In that place they used to give you three Woodbine cigarettes every day even though you were only ten!"

As we sit on Maxine's step and chat one morning, she lists the names of all of the families that have already left the block and all of those, including herself, that have still to go. She sits on the high part of the step, wrapped in a long, red dressing gown with her hair tied back, drinking tea from a red chipped mug and smoking a cigarette. She usually has her phone in her hand, seeking or sending information. She has told me before that she wants a 'house', and when I ask her why, she tells me that "the flats are not the same anymore, people used to look after each other when we were growing up now they just rat on you". She makes reference to a children's party that had been organised by residents of the block to mark 'the end' of the block and that "someone had called the old bill". On many other occasions she contradicts this and displays strong affection for the estate when she says, "Even with the drink and the drugs there was a great community here." She now has two young children of her own whose care needs dominate her life most of the time between pre-school and school and looking after them. She describes going to school in a local religious-run primary school and says they refused her access to the secondary school and she then ended up in the vocational secondary school. She had a spell as a care worker on a community employment scheme that she says finished as soon as the scheme finished, saying "It wasn't much good anyway because you were only getting 20 euros on top of your benefit."

We are joined on the step by Michelle, a neighbour who lives in a flat on a balcony some floors above Maxine and who stops off for a smoke and a chat before her shift in a Dublin hospital. They talk about how things are changing and the emptying-out of the block and what it will mean for both of them. They are apprehensive as to what will happen. Maxine's desire to leave is juxtaposed against Michelle's will to stay. Both of their families have long histories here, with Michelle's grandparents being original tenants when the estate first opened. Michelle's mother, just like Maxine's, left the estate and was given a council house some years ago. Both of them say that their mothers would come back tomorrow if they could and have never really gotten used to living off the estate in houses. I am to hear this directly from Maxine's mother on the step one day when she derides her daughter's wish to leave the estate for a house and her lack of understanding of the isolation by saying "Why did I leave? There's only me and the dog in the house. ... Wait until she leaves, she won't know what hit her, there'll be no sitting on the step then." This theme of how Maxine will manage when she leaves was also picked up by one of her close friends, Rosy, who would often come for a chat and a smoke on the step. In a similar vein to Maxine's mother, she says one day "she won't be fuckin able for it, she won't be able to handle it. She loves the chat and the sittin out and the info that goes around. She won't be able to do without that." Rosy's logic is that for someone who has been at the centre of things it will be difficult to leave and to move into a house and know no one. The conversation turns to the paid employment that the women have done over the years. Maxine has worked as a carer in a large institutional care home for adults and children and was able to complete a childcare training course as part of her community employment scheme. Michelle has worked first in the canteen and then on the wards of a hospital for a number of years now. Low-paid work is paralleled by the heavier burden of unpaid family and childcare work that both of them spend huge energy trying to manage as best they can. Michelle relies heavily on her best friend, Sonya, for childcare support, as does Maxine on her sister. Both of them also live in the block. Michelle is pregnant and is due her third child soon. The summer heat is taking its toll on her now as she walks from the estate to work and back. "I would love a job like yours," she says to me on one particularly hot August day.

Like all of the other people to move, both of them are now caught up in a housing process and are unsure as to what will happen. This process is mediated for all residents by the on-site council housing manager who rings people or calls to their homes and tells them of housing possibilities either on or off site in other locations. He controls all of the information on what offers are available and who should and will get them and in what order. He often turns up in the block, surveying the scene. One of the unusual things about this period is that because there is pressure to move everybody out so that the reconstruction can begin, we see a somewhat speeded-up version of the usually slow-moving public housing allocations system. Maxine and Michelle and a whole range of other people are trying to navigate their way to good housing outcomes for themselves and their families. On one hand, they are perhaps lucky in that they happen to be resident in the blocks where the process is beginning and will have quicker outcomes than those in the later phases. They are luckier than those who will have to wait for a much longer period to move.

And yet, all of this takes place within a field in which they have very little power or control as to where they end up or what housing they get. They have no power to buy and no consciousness of the private housing field or what it entails. There is also a dialectical tension between the current rising value of a public housing tenancy, given the scarcity of public housing and the more general and deliberate devaluing of public housing in the mind of the general public over recent years. The fact that the options they have are within a very small section of the more general housing field is taken for granted. At different times both of them are told by the estate manager of places that might be available. On one occasion Maxine is offered a house in poor condition in another part of the city, which she rejects outright, and says, "I am not going there." Michelle, who has very clearly a wish to stay in the estate, is told by the estate manager to go and view an apartment off site being run by a voluntary housing association, and she does, but it comes to nothing in the end. The attempt at realising one's preferences is at the heart of this phase of people moving within and without the estate. Preferences are built on the elements of location, quality, size and the overall attractiveness of a dwelling and an area to residents. If they are thinking of moving out and not coming back, as Maxine has declared, preferences usually follow tacit lines of class-cultural continuity laid down in the past. These preferences are strictly conditioned by what is available and where. Within the limitations of what is on offer, Maxine has a preference for areas in relatively close proximity that are historically working class and culturally familiar and appeal to her as places where she would want to live, and make sense for her in relation to her children's schooling. At one point she hears of a house being offered to someone else and she tells me that the family who lived in the house previously "were burned out" and there is no way she would take it. Michelle has also heard these stories, and when she is offered this house, she also turns it down. Michelle says that she is worried that if she moves out of the estate and "gives out to young people" in a place where no one knows her she will have no back-up or support of neighbours. The realisation or non-realisation of preferences is governed by what is available and what is offered, but is also heavily influenced by what is acceptable to people. Even though residents had been told by council officials that the council would purchase houses as part of the process, in effect almost no new stock was purchased and almost all of the units offered to residents came from existing city council stock. There was therefore a very small pool of housing available. To compensate for this lack the council also sourced housing units from a voluntary housing body to house people off the estate. There is much pressure on the council therefore to rehouse people so that the demolition and construction work can begin as soon as possible.

A few days later, on an adjacent step, Maxine and Michelle and other women have a heated conversation about how these issues work and as to how the whole system works, which they confess to themselves that they don't understand. Nearly all of the women smoke as they talk. They have all been asked to attend meetings individually with city council officials to discuss their housing needs and possibilities. All of the women are generally apprehensive about these meetings, and they say that council officials are much nicer to them when the local community workers attend. Beneath the surface of the conversation is a desire, as well as for good personal outcomes, for fairness and transparency as to how the whole thing works. Maxine's sister Emily has just come from one of these meetings and has in her hand a green form that she says she has been told to fill in, because to be officially registered on the 'transfer list' this is a necessity. She has been told that she 'must bring it to the Tax Office', for reasons that she doesn't understand. Later it transpires that it is to ensure she holds no other assets or property that would undermine her eligibility for public housing. Other women on the step say that they have not had to do this, and it must be a new thing. The women ream off the names of people from those who must move and who have been made offers in other parts of the city, and of the 'list' that determines who is next in line to get a move. Clare, around whose step people are gathered, says there is confusion between the 'general transfer list' in the city council and the 'local list' that exists just for the people within the estate who have to move out of Blocks A and B to facilitate the work to be done. Emily says that she is ninth on this local list to move now. Michelle joins the conversation as she comes into the block after just finishing her meeting with the city council and tells everyone that they have told her that she is fourth on this local list. I am told by them all that it is the length of one's tenancy that is most important in this transition process. How long you have been a tenant is cross-referenced by housing need, which is determined by family size. The larger the family, the larger the housing unit needed.

There is a conversation about a man who was given a flat off site by a voluntary housing association and some of the women ask why he got a two-bedroom apartment, given that he was only recently given his own tenancy by the council. The inference is that he should not have got this move so soon. Through the sharing of knowledge and information on this local grapevine people are keenly aware as to who is moving, when and where. There is continuous assessment and verification as to one's position and priority within the whole process. There is also a continuous updating on who has moved and where they have gone. While people may not activate their critique formally, they do critique what they see as unfairness. Maxine asks is there a specific two-bed list, and how does that work? She says that because she is a single parent with two male children she is entitled only to a 'two-bed', as the two male children can share a bedroom. Clare, around whose step the gathering is taking place, has been offered a three-bedroom flat within the estate in another block that is located on the top floor and that requires climbing and descending eight flights of stairs, as there is no lift. She has rejected it because she just wouldn't be able to manage the stairs "with four kids and a grandchild, the shopping and everything else". She says "that might suit you Michelle".

Janet, another of the women present, has been a tenant for over three decades and has been in a dispute with the council for some months now. This is because the council have refused to let her put her son 'back on the rent' after he had been in prison for a brief period, during which time she had taken him off to reduce her own financial burden. This means he is officially homeless. As part of the transition process, she had applied to be housed off the estate by the same housing association as others, but her application was rejected. This has happened to a small number of other people as well. These issues dominated Janet's life for much of this period and brought to the surface not so much the fact that (informal) sanctions operate but that when they do there is little or no explanation as to why or how they do. Janet was so distressed about it that she discussed it with a solicitor because she felt that her rights as a tenant were being breached. She had said to me on another occasion "Fuck them. After so many years [resident and tenant] I am not having that when other people get sorted. What's wrong with me?" The effects of the process were not lost on the son in question, who had mocked the official regeneration discourse, saying to me one day, "yeah, yeah, all this regeneration, keeping families together, keeping communities together". Janet's recourse to formal legal support was taken because of the council's refusal to engage with her. In the midst of this process, she bemoaned to me one day, "With all the talk of homelessness on the telly you'd think they would just let him on 'the floor' [the rent], and not have another one in cardboard city."

Lauren is another of the women present and lives across the block. She has just had a new baby and has her in her arms. She was one of a group of people that campaigned to have the estate refurbished and regenerated. She has stepped back from that now and is worried about what will happen to herself and her own family. She is an assertive woman and is confident that she will get a good housing outcome, and expresses a strong desire to come back even if the family leaves the estate temporarily. Her steely resolve, however, has been sorely tested by the sight of a large rat entering a drain close to her flat in recent days. Lauren managed to return to education through the local college that provided adult education, and from this went on to complete a degree in a prestigious Dublin university that provided her with a qualification to gain employment in a state agency. She was very much the exception to the rule and was one of the handful of people that I came across in the estate who had accessed the third-level education system. She has told me that colleagues at work would ask her why she was still living in the public housing system and, given she now had a salaried position, shouldn't she be buying her own house?

Block A slowly empties over time. There is a crew of men in a white box truck who carry out all of the moves. They are careful to wrap everything, using metre-wide cellophane rolls of stretchy plastic. Occasionally there are problems getting furniture into and out of flats. Clare's sofa won't fit when she moves from Block A to Block E temporarily. New insulation has slightly reduced the door frame sizes making it impossible one day to get a sofa in. Every flat that is vacated is shuttered up within days, using brown, rusty steel sheets to stop vandalism or squatting or the theft of valuable copper cylinders and the flooding that follows. Sound and movement diminish almost to zero as life gradually seeps out of the place. Lives are put into boxes in the hope of something better. Because she wants to leave the estate, Maxine is one of the last to go, given the difficulties of finding houses within the public housing system outside of the estate. She says that more and more rats are emerging. "Real ones John," she says. Others tell me that the rats know that the people have gone and are coming looking for food. I arrive at Maxine's flat one morning and the last of her few possessions have been loaded into a white van. She has been given a two-bedroom council house in an old working-class estate a short distance away. She gets into the van and, as she is closing the door, says "I am happy with what I got."

3

Work ethic 1

Frank

'Some of the older men doing the shuttering have asked me, they said "Frank, what happened in this country? How did things get like this and so bad so quickly?" The fact that workers don't even get travel time. Even '——' didn't do that when the bad times came, they still paid workers their travel time. Young people today don't understand how terms and conditions had to be fought for and won and took a lot of time and effort.' (Frank)

Frank's flat is sparsely furnished but it is scrupulously clean both inside and outside. He has painted the entire exterior balcony from floor to ceiling that provides access to his and two other flats. The paintwork of emulsion with white gloss fringe is sharp and crisp and to a high standard. Things are the same on the inside, where the flat is neat and spartan. It displays a level of care and attention to detail that is central to Frank's sense of himself and how work is supposed to get done. It stands out against the background of general decay that characterises the block. He has been separated for a period of years and lives on his own in a flat in Bridgetown. He has worked in construction for most of his life, although he had a period after he left school, working for a large retailer in one of their stores. He is now well into his fifties. Along with a group of other men from the estate he did a recent pre-employment course that includes the mandatory 'safe pass' that every worker needs to have to work on construction sites in Ireland. The course was organised by the local employment agency in order to help men from the Bridgetown Estate obtain work in construction. When I first make contact with Frank in 2017 he has been unemployed for over five years, after the almost total disintegration of the construction industry in Ireland. Prior to this, Frank had worked for a large construction company for a number of years. He describes it as a company with good pay and conditions. He had also attained a degree of control over his labour and was accorded a level of trust and respect within the company, due to his experience. He was usually sent to sort out the many snags that had to be repaired when a site was nearing completion for handover. When the financial crisis began, things changed quickly and he ended up in the labour court with his employer, trying to secure redundancy. He achieved a modest settlement that many of the other construction workers in the company were able to avail themselves of, due to his efforts. The crash has meant that there has been little or no work to speak of for over five or six years now. Frank has been involved in workers' unions and strike actions and knows that good conditions did not exist because of the good nature of the contractor but were due mainly to efforts of previous generations of workers, including himself. His sense of identity and self-respect is built on his concept of himself as a hard worker who is assiduous in his commitment that things be done properly on sites. This has often led to his frustration with younger men, some of whom he sees as having neither the capacity to work as hard nor an understanding of the nature of class relations they find themselves enmeshed in as workers.

In 2017 the first part of the construction of the new housing on the estate begins. Frank has watched the work begin and actively sought work on the site as it took off, but initially with no success. There was good support from local community projects as well as local employment services, but, as he often says, contractors are very picky when it comes to whom they hire. In the early stages of the construction process he watches on in frustration at what he sees as dubious practices where bricklayers are labouring for themselves, and explains to me that the contractor is reducing the overall cost to themselves and increasing the workload on individual workers. Frank asks me in frustration, "Why they don't employ labourers now?" As we look at the site together, he points out how this is happening but says that it will be difficult for the contractor to sustain this practice as the site goes up above ground level and gets more complicated. He continues to press his claim for work on the site and eventually gets a job in the middle of 2017, labouring for bricklayers. He is initially happy to be working again, but the onerous physical demands of the work immediately press down on him and bring him to a realisation that, given the nature of the work, time may be against him. Body diverges from will, and on one of many visits to his flat he shows me blistered hands and bruised arms and describes the toll the work is taking on him and says he has probably been over-working to prove a point to himself and his new employers that he is still well able to do the work. Within a short period of starting, however, the demands of the work and the poor rewards are visible to him. As we have a cup of tea in his flat one evening he tells me:

'the work on the site is too hard, it's not the way it used to be … the brickies are layin 400 blocks a day each, that's 800 blocks and those first-level blocks, the Newtons [special blocks for ground-level construction] are a bastard weight. When they get to the second level the blocks are not as heavy. But you have to run here, run there, getting them ties, wettin the boards, puttin mortar up and movin along the line all the time. The wages are fucked now compared to what they used to be. All the blokes on the site are sayin it. When I worked for '——' I used to get a decent wage, now it's all just work work work, there's no let-up.' (Frank)

By carefully managing himself, Frank readapts to the work slowly over the initial weeks. He has various creams, ointments and powders on the coffee table in the sitting room that will soothe and salve the parts of his body that are raw from the work. A bone in his back is causing him problems where there is a bone spur that he has tried to have rectified recently by paying privately to see a consultant for an assessment because, as he says, he couldn't stand the pain any longer and knew that in the public health system it would be a long time before he got an appointment. The unevenness of the ground on site is also causing him problems with his feet. When he first starts back his body is so shattered by Friday that he needs the entire weekend to rest and recover. These first few days and weeks on the site are a period of abrupt physical readjustment to the world of construction, but also are a realisation that things have changed in other ways as well. There are other issues compounding the physical. Over a period of time, Frank discovers that the financial return for one's efforts has also undergone a metamorphosis. The main contractor has subcontracted all of the block laying and brick work to another company, and in Frank's estimation the effect of their lowest-bid strategy is the acute physical and financial exploitation of workers like himself. Labour costs must be kept to a minimum, he says. From the start he is concerned at the fact that he is not given pay slips and cannot get a straight answer as to how his pay is structured and what tax will be paid on his behalf. On a day soon after he has started he says "the builder gave me 500 euros after tax [for a five day week] but I was getting much better money when I was with ——. He said to me 'that's what we pay Frank'." Some weeks later, during a week when there was a bank holiday and the site was closed for a second day due to heavy rain, Frank finds that his wages have gone down from 500 to 300 for the week.

'I didn't mind when they didn't pay me for the first bank holiday because I didn't have enough hours worked up, but now if they don't pay me after being with them for the past weeks. No, they have given me nothing like that and when you think of the need for housing and hospitals here and the amount of tax that is not being paid it's out of order.' (Frank)

Frank has little difficulty making the connection between overall taxation contributions and the funding and provision of public services. The contractor is placing the payment of tax burden on the worker and is paying them substantially less than before the crisis. Frank was so irritated and worried by this that he visited the department of revenue on a number of occasions to ensure he wouldn't be penalised for non-payment of tax after the work ended. There was an inspection of the site, but in Frank's view those in political power were only interested in reducing the numbers on the unemployment register and had no real interest in the nature of work, how people were treated or what they were paid.

He finds himself in a changed post-recession landscape and discovers that things are not the way they once were, and that in this changed labour regime workers are now being treated as self-employed, individualised work units where they no longer receive the entitlements or benefits that were standard not so long ago. This includes things like having an entitlement to sick pay and to holiday pay. Both he and other young men who come to work on the same site are paid €100 a day but are not paid for bank holidays or for rained-off days or if they are sick for any reason. If they take holidays, they are not paid. Frank explains to me on a number of occasions that such entitlements must come out of the weekly wage they are receiving and that workers, without direction, must somehow understand this and budget their own money to allocate enough resources for these things. Frank knows that this is not the norm, but it appears as the natural order of things for younger men who are having their first real experience of the construction industry. As he points out to me, when all of these things are taken into account, the real value of the weekly wage will decrease significantly and workers will discover that they are earning not much above the minimum wage for very demanding work. This would be the real rate of pay, it seems. In his flat one evening Frank produces a pamphlet from the union that outlines the pay rates that manual workers, both skilled and unskilled, are supposed to receive. He hands it to me and laughs at the text as he puts it on the coffee table. It is a new version of individualisation, with the end of maximising exploitation and control on the part of the contractor. Frank is class conscious and is well aware of these issues. He had been a strike leader in a previous life in a large company and was asked at that time to speak on platforms at radical left-wing conferences. He attended but didn't speak, preferring to immerse himself in the work and action of the strike.

Some of the other men who also did the pre-employment course are also seeking work. Two of them are offered places on a training course outside Dublin that will show them how to install dry-wall sheeting, plasterboard and insulation. I meet them often in different parts of the estate as they hang out, sometimes smoking weed. They are excited by the prospect of going beyond the city they know and experiencing something different. Two of them, Sean and Eddie (another of the group, Lawrence, pulls out at the last minute), begin the training course and are given an induction period and then begin the official training programme. A few weeks into the programme, Sean returns to Dublin and decides not to go back. Eddie, on the other hand, sticks out the course but has a dispute with a foreman on his first proper job when he returns to Dublin and drops out of the training programme soon after. I learn this as these work stories and updates are often shared, impromptu, at various places in the estate. When Sean explains to me and Frank one morning that he has given up the training, Frank is frustrated at Sean's lack of understanding of the importance of work. Looking at me he says, "He fucked it up down there, didn't he?" referring to the training course. Soon after, he makes a case to the contractor to hire Sean, which the contractor does. Not long after this Eddie also begins work on the site. Sean is thrown straight into work with bricklayers on the site. Working for bricklayers puts a challenge to young men like Sean to prove themselves up to the task. This theme of masculinity and of proving oneself physically capable to meet such demands is strong. While Frank's physical powers are waning, Sean's are at their peak. He is powerfully built and frequents the local gym every couple of days. On one occasion on a hot summer's day as he and Eddie and others are cooking food unsuccessfully on a small barbecue, he tells me of his high-protein diet and where he sources top-quality meat for a good price. He is by far the physically strongest of all of his peer group and some of the others find that they cannot physically do what he can do. Eddie, for instance, gets a job doing more general labouring on the site. Sean takes to this work without a problem and is soon 'running the line' for two bricklayers, providing them with bricks, mortar, sills, ties and anything else they need. On days when I meet him as he finishes, he points out the various parts of the site he is working on and says he has no problems keeping up.

Sean seems happy to be able to find a way to express his immense physical strength, yet still retains a clear desire to do work that is interesting and provocative and more financially rewarding. One day, after coming off a shift on the site in full work gear, covered in a grey dust, he tells me, "I want something behind me and not to end up labourin for the rest of me life. I'll do this for a while but it's not for good." Another of this peer group, Lawrence, has started work on the same site with a scaffolding crew, but is soon disillusioned with the rates of pay. Outside the local shop he expresses his frustration to me and tells me he is on €320 a week, which is just over €60 a day, of which he says "That's not much more than the minimum wage." He is trying to negotiate a better wage for himself and tells me that there is some potential within the scaffolding field for better wages. Lawrence doesn't remain long on the site and finds what he says is a better-paid job, working in construction closer to the city.

Frank is let go by the contractor after a period of six to seven months, with the promise of more work to come on other sites. Frank is sceptical about the offer and reads it as a way of easing him out the door and making sure there are no more questions asked about the pay and conditions on offer. Sean and Eddie remain on the site for a little while longer, but they are also let go quite soon after Frank. It is clear that for Frank the work contract is no longer valid for him as a fair exchange of labour for wage. He has long ago penetrated the real nature of the work relationship and the brutality of it. This is brought home sharply to Frank and the others when a worker is injured by a machine on the site one day and this is soon followed by the death of a man who has a heart attack and has to be taken down from the scaffolding in the bucket of a machine. These incidents have a strong effect on Frank, and also on Sean and Eddie. Frank thinks that it might have been one of the lads that was injured and is worried, but is relieved when he finds out it isn't. He speaks of other sites: "I have been on site when blokes have been killed and the whole place goes silent and the blokes say nothing." Frank now seeks work that is less onerous and with better conditions and that will perhaps offer him a little bit more dignity in the final years of his paid working life. "I'm done with the building work. Where do I go now? What do I do now? I have put in applications to the hospitals but have heard nothing back so far."

Just as Frank advocated for the young men to be employed on the site, he also advocated for skilled men, one of whom was a bricklayer and who was given a job on the site on the back of Frank's recommendation. But there remains a tension between skilled and unskilled men, and Frank often talks about the particular relationship between skilled and unskilled men on sites. There is often resentment from labourers that bricklayers get to do more interesting and stimulating work and get paid more, while labourers must serve them. Frank describes a number of examples where some bricklayers are disrespectful to labourers and on occasion undermine them in front of the site foreman to display their more powerful position in the labour hierarchy. And yet, while they may be better paid than labourers, bricklayers have not been spared the effects of austerity either. The weekly wage for bricklayers on the site was €700, and they were subject to exactly the same practices of pay and conditions whereby they were not paid for holiday leave, sick leave or bank holidays or wet days, just like the labourers. Given their skills, however, and the shortage of skilled tradesmen, they were more in demand, while labourers could be discarded and replaced at will from the reserve army of labour.

In mid-2018, while I am walking through the estate, I meet Frank, who finished on the site some months ago. He is engrossed in conversation with another of the men who also did the pre-employment course, Conor. Conor had been employed on a large building project in the city and seemed to have gotten the longest period of employment of any of those who had done the pre-employment course. He is chatting animatedly to Frank when I arrive and is in a very agitated state. He tells the story again for my benefit and says that the contractor let him go just a couple of weeks short of two years working for them. "You know why that is," he says, "cos they wouldn't have to give me any redundancy, so they made sure to get rid of me." Frank is surprised and not surprised to hear this. "I thought you were alright there," he says, "but then after what happened to us on the other site sure you can't trust any of the cunts anymore." Conor says that it wasn't the site foreman who gave him the news but a much more senior person from within the company who arrived on the site and picked out five or six people and told them all they would be finishing that week. Conor describes asking him "But sure the work is not finished, why would you be letting us go?" He says the foreman responded by telling him and the others, "Look lads, it's nothing personal, it's just that you haven't got the tickets or the skills that we need for the next stage, so that's it." Conor describes 'losing the head' with the man and then asking his own foreman who responded by saying, "I knew nothing about it. I'm really sorry about that Conor." Conor goes on to say that "and after us a few days later they brought 30 Romanians on to the site. I mean fuck, that it's as clear as day." There is no way to verify this. At this stage a friend of Conor's arrives at the step who has been working in a large factory for some years now. He says that the company paid for him to update his forklift ticket and he was doing the training today. When he listens to the conversation about what happened to Conor he simply says, "Sure the construction is fucked. Why would you bother your bollox with that?" Conor says back to him, "You better get me a job in your place, I'm going to look for factory work now, fuck that construction."

All of the men from the estate who did the safe-pass course got work on construction sites, but all were finished within relatively short time spans. For Frank, Sean and Eddie the work lasted between six and nine months, while for men like Conor it was slightly longer. On this occasion they are all generally disillusioned with construction and say there has been little or no work since they finished. There are other construction sites beginning close to the estate, but Frank has lost all interest in looking for work on them. He goes back to the local employment service and gets a more up-to-date CV done and is still dreaming of a hospital porter's job that seems unlikely. His will to work and to be useful is undiminished, but it seems there is little outlet that would offer him a dignified end to his paid working career. On the most recent occasion I meet him he is now participating in the local 'Men's Shed' project and tells me he is going on a trip to the west of Ireland.

Karl

'That's not what we were put here for is it?' (Karl)

'I could go on forever but to sum up it's just not for me, like it's not, it's not for me. ... I feel like I've got a lot more to offer. And certainly working in – it's not what I feel I should be doing.' (Karl)

When I first meet Karl to sit down and talk, he has just moved off the estate to facilitate the reconstruction of the older blocks, one of which he had moved into not too long before. He had recently moved out of his mother's flat and had been allocated a flat of his own on the estate. This made him a tenant in his own right. Within a short period of his moving in, the council were asking him to move out again because the block he had moved into was to be demolished as part of the physical reconstruction. As part of this transition, he was housed with an approved housing body in a nearby estate where he was allocated a two-bedroom flat because this estate contained no one-bedroom flats. Luck and timing are important in Karl's story, as his swift progression through the housing system is in contrast to that of his mother, who will not move until a later phase and will therefore have to wait a considerable period of time to be rehoused. In his new flat his rent is €240 a month. The reason it is low is because tenants of council housing pay what is known as a 'differential rent' up to a maximum of 15% of total household income. He readily acknowledges the value of this to him in many ways. He is acutely aware of what people are paying in the same area in the private rented sector. He tells me a story of a work colleague who is paying €1,500 a month for a similar apartment in the private rented sector very close to his and asks, "What's that all about? I am so lucky." This succinct statement encapsulates a whole host of issues that arise around the nature and provision and cost of housing.

Karl's paid work life started as a part-time lounge boy in one of the area's local pubs, and he was offered work behind the bar when he was still in school. As he describes it, "I was makin €150 a week plus the tips I was getting. Not bad for a 15-year-old young fella." He had a strong sense that he was good at business from his time in secondary school, but says that his teachers discouraged him from taking it as a subject and had little belief in him. On a general level he says that he didn't like secondary school, and tells me in detail why he thought the standard of teaching and the school itself were both in poor condition. Even though he didn't formally study business at second level, he decided to go in and do the Leaving Cert business exam, and received what he describes as a very good grade for someone who hadn't been studying the subject formally. His hope was to develop this acumen after school by starting with a business course in a Post Leaving Certificate course after he had finished his secondary schooling, and then progressing from there. Not long after leaving school, however, he started working for a large company in one of their local stores. In his first two years there he worked as a general assistant, and he was then promoted to the position of junior manager. He describes this transition in the following way: "It's very easy in a place like '—', to get a management role, once you work hard, like, you know that way. Because they notice, like. So I was working, I was working really hard and someone approached me about moving up to management level and I was like yeah." In this new post he is a key holder and has responsibilities to open the store at 5.30 in the morning when the deliveries arrive and to make sure that everything is stacked properly and to ensure that what is supposed to be delivered actually arrives. He tells me a story one day about a delivery man trying to short-change him on a delivery by giving less than he should have, but he was sharp enough to see through 'the stroke'. He also has a new position of authority over people who were formerly equals to him. He doesn't seem to like the authority. "I would never really have to tell anyone what to do. I'd just have to make sure it's done, do you know what I mean?" When I first meet Karl, he has been working there for almost seven years and he describes how, when he first started, he had other dreams for himself and his future beyond working in the local store. He reflects on the distance between what he wanted to do or might have done and what he actually ended up doing and the difficulty of trying to get from one to the other.

Karl: I was going to go to '—' college to do something, something to do with business anyway.
JB: And did you go?
Karl: No because I ended up getting a job with '—'. I ended up working. I ended up because I was so desperate for a job, you know what I mean like. I says to myself, ah! college can wait, like you know, I'll work for a year, I'll save a few bob and everything else I said and then I'll go to college next year like, but it didn't happen. I just couldn't, I just couldn't take myself away from it. You know what I mean like. Money, it was decent you know, what I mean like, money is decent. It's not, it's not the job I want to be in but I was earning a decent few bob, you know for a 17-year-old young fella like. And I was like, ah the following year I was like, I'll go and then I never went, and then the following year I was definitely going and never went, and still to this day like.

Despite the fact that he was given a promotion and more responsibility early in the job, it hasn't turned out to be what he had hoped for. Over time, Karl has become frustrated and disillusioned in the store. "I want to use my brain," he tells me repeatedly as we sit one day in a local pub having a sandwich discussing all of this. He has realised that not only is it difficult to change direction and to reorient oneself along or across work tracks, but the work is also destroying him psychologically. He has discovered that there is no correlation between his natural capacities and the job he finds himself in. This theme of not being fulfilled and wasting away recurs, and he repeats the phrase many times: "Me brain is wasted in there. I am being wasted in there." In our first meeting he had expressed similar sentiments, saying, "It's not for me, like it's not, it's not for me, like I feel like I have a lot more to offer." Karl's account of his work expresses a desire to be doing something else, but he finds it hard to put his finger on exactly what it is that he wants. He often says that it's not money that interests or motivates him. Yet he has some attachment to the idea of the status of a job in the overall occupational structure. He is offended on occasion by the 'the scumbags' who come into the shop trying to rob stuff or asking people for a 'shot' of their mobile phones, only to run off with them. He is attracted to the idea of working in a bank and often calls upon the image of a friend of his who is an accountant, a job he admires. He expresses a desire to work in banking but finds no opportunities when he searches online for jobs that might suit, and says, "Only 10 per cent of the jobs apply to me because all of the others require degree-level qualifications." When I come into the shop one day he comes out of the back office and asks me to find out how he would go about going to college and how he could afford it. While talking to me he smiles and reminds me gently, "I have the rent to pay and stuff like that, you know." I come back a few days later and give him the information and he processes it, but later tells me that he feels that he isn't able to act on it at this time in his life. His inner frustration reflects the tension between the material necessity of earning a wage and the desire to flourish as a sensuous being and to do interesting work.

Karl seems more content and happier than someone like Frank when it comes to what he earns by way of a wage. When I ask him about what he is paid, he says, "It's enough money, yeah ... when I say decent for the amount of work I do like, like today was a rough old day in work, I'd a lot to do today. But on a general basis I wouldn't, I wouldn't have an awful lot of work ... there's a bit of office work involved and stuff like that in what I do and it's not a very, it's not a very strenuous job like that, so when I say the money is decent, for what I do, do you know what I mean?"

And yet, at another level Karl has absorbed through conversations and information the downward evolution of the pay structure in the organisation over a period of time. He knows that what people earn today is far lower than what they earned in the past. But for Karl that's just the way it is. He describes these redistributive events as they relate to people and to generations that have preceded him and as if they have little or nothing to do with him. They are discrete events, somewhere back in historical time, and in his mind his time and the conditions he works under are a separate container to those of previous generations of workers. He says that older staff members have said to him "before the recession it was great, we were earning great money". He describes the chronology of wage depression over a period of two decades in the following way:

'Like before 2007 if you got taken on in – you were taken on at let's say a tenner an hour. And you could move up as high as, if you stayed long enough, you could move up as high as seventeen euros an hour. There's a girl I work with and she's here before 2006 and she is on close to 17 euros an hour, so that is a very decent wage, do you know what I mean? Now the last few years the contracts that they're giving to people, you can go up to 12 euro an hour and never go any further, unless you move up to management … and then going back even further like, you know, if you're in — since before 1996 21 euro an hour, imagine that. I swear to you, it's no word of a lie.' (Karl)

People on these older, higher wage rates appear like strange oddities to Karl, and the company has taken action to try to remove them all en masse through various strategies, including large-scale redundancy. What was normal just over 20 years ago appears almost unthinkable when we talk. As Karl described earlier, today the starting hourly rate for a general assistant is much lower and is capped at €12 an hour. People on these older contracts are like artefacts from a time past. Just like Sean and Eddie, Karl has, as of yet, no consciousness as to how conditions and wages were fought for and how they came into being. I chat to him one day about the union campaign to stop the company taking action against them to remove those people on older contracts, and he is indifferent to it, preferring to focus on trying to find his own way out of the company. His answer to the problem of not being fulfilled at work is to seek work for another company. The prospect of trying to re-enter the field of education diminishes as time passes. The difficulties of managing financially are crucial for Karl, and he feels that he would not be able to survive if he didn't have some means to support himself while returning to education. He tells me this as he is checking out someone's groceries at the till one day. He also tells me that he has secured a job with a large media company in their tele-sales department and has decided to pack it in where he is now.

4

Work ethic 2

Michelle

'I have had [a] good life even though I have had a hard life. You know, I don't look back and think oh why me or anything. It's just the hand you are dealt, I guess. One way you can look at it is as being a good hand, you know, and then others, they can say well its [a] bad hand, but it's just life. You have to get on with it and deal with it.' (Michelle)

Just like Frank and many others in Bridgetown and beyond, Michelle's family have not been spared the effects of the crash and the austerity of recent years. In response to a question about her family history on the estate Michelle tells me unprompted of her father's redundancy during the recession. She describes the intergenerational effects of the crisis on her father after he lost his job with little or no prospect of other work. While Frank tells his own narrative directly, Michelle speaks of her father's redundancy in the second person, as a daughter looking in on her father from the outside as his sense of self and identity received a traumatic shock. She expresses a strong and innate sense of injustice at the fact that someone like her father, who wants to work, will have great difficulty finding any real function in society, given that, like Frank, he is leaning toward the wrong end of the age spectrum in work terms. He too worked in construction, but the only thing on offer to him at this stage is a 'Back to Work Scheme' that the government developed and promoted as a response to the crisis. As she describes it, with implicit reference to the class structure:

'Me father worked hard all his life you know, and they paid their taxes and whatever and then unfortunately was made redundant. Due to the recession like, and then has to claim the dole and is made to go on this programme, because he is a hard-working man like, and that's the thanks they get for all the years and paying their taxes and you know, coming from a low-cost low-class area or whatever they call it. It's unfair like, it's very unfair because they do graft hard.' (Michelle)

Michelle's life trajectory has some similarities with Karl's in that she also started working in local pubs when she was a young teenager. But, in contrast to Karl, Michelle has had the added burden of having had a child in her late teens and of trying to navigate parenthood and finding a place to live off the estate before being rehoused back on the estate after four years in private rented accommodation. She has spent most of her time parenting as a single parent, but has a partner in her life in recent years. She talks about not having much money growing up and of feeling this going to school, when classmates had more than she did, and she noticed and felt this lack:

'I wouldn't have had a lot growing up, do you know what I mean? And other people in the class would have, say, they went in with a pencil case, where I would have had one pencil. You know and you feel a little inadequate, that's kind of what I felt growing up in that school. People would have had their lunches made where I would have had to eat the [school] lunch.' (Michelle)

She went to a mixed-gender secondary school with only a small number of girls, and she felt this helped her to focus on the schoolwork, because she felt, as one of only two girls in the class, that she didn't want to be noticed. As she describes, "You just put your head down and become this good student, where if I had been with a group of girls, I probably would have been the messer of the class." She completed her Leaving Certificate and, although she was very committed to her schooling, she says that she wasn't naturally gifted and had to work twice as hard as her sole female fellow student in the class, for whom the academic work seemed to come so easily. She says that she was really good at woodwork at school, and in her final years also became very good at technical drawing, prompting one of her teachers to suggest to her that she should think of doing a course in this field.

After finishing the Leaving Certificate, and on the advice of the careers guidance counsellor, she went on to do a Post Leaving Certificate in Business Studies and says that she still can't explain why she did this course. She had completed all of the classes but didn't do the final exams because she had her first child at this time. Her recollection of this moment is one of dejection and utter resignation: "Because I was pregnant I don't know if it was hormones or what, I just kind of went oh fuck. My life is fucked so." After she had the baby, she found poor rental accommodation not too far from the estate, but, in her mind, she wanted to get back to the estate as soon as she could. She says that she knows there are risks for children growing up in Bridgetown (more than once she says she doesn't want her daughter roaming the streets), but she has a deep attachment to the place that draws her back. "I fought for ages and ages to get back. The whole system like. And eventually I got it." In the current process of change on the estate she has been ruminating on what is best for herself and her children: "You know, I didn't want to leave, but I was thinking, you have that doubt, are you making the right decision here or is this your opportunity to make a kind of better life?" This existential dilemma, which occurs for so many people, is acute, but she reasons out her own logic that for her it is better to stay than to go:

> 'but I don't think it is making a better life for your kids, I don't think it matters where you live. It's a true saying. It's how you live. Because I see moves outside the flats and to be honest there are families that have went on drugs, they have had problems you know, probably much more worse problems than I would have had living in Bridgetown. So I will just stick it and stay here. I love the community.' (Michelle)

She has a view that her conditions of life may undergo little change even if she moves off the estate. In her own risk assessment, there are more good things than bad things, in that there are also risks in being housed elsewhere, including isolation and removal from social and family networks. She has a large family tree that she traces back to when the estate was first built and her grandparents moved in as original tenants. And even though she thinks the estate has changed, with people being less social these days, the goods far outweigh the bads for her. Michelle has been working since her early teens doing different jobs, starting in pubs and hotels. The need to have some money of her own and some sense of independence was pushing her in this direction from when she was barely a teenager.

Michelle:	I worked since I'm 13. So I would have worked from first year on, if you like.
JB:	And what kind of work were you doing?
Michelle:	I worked as a lounge girl and then I would have took up a bit of cleaning and I have always earned a bit of money. And then when I was 16 I worked for the summer in a hotel in Temple Bar doing the housekeeping. And when I went back to school I would have done it at weekends, it was a time when I was actually doing my Leaving Cert at the time. I done lounge girl at the weekends and still went to school like.

Within a short period of her first child being born Michelle got a job working in a Dublin hospital in the canteen–restaurant. The work involved, as she says, "serving food, doing the wash up, cleaning the floor, putting out salad bowls". She also did some basic training in manual handling and in food hygiene. Her mother looked after her children while she was working. As she discusses her approach to work it becomes evident that, in a similar vein to Karl and Frank, a strong work ethic is central to her sense of herself and her sense of self-worth and dignity. "I think, to be fair, coming from Bridgetown it gives you a stronger work ethic. You know, you go into work and you do your work, and where I have had people come into work and they think they get paid to do nothing."

This extends into her frustration with the hospital for not replacing staff in the restaurant who were out sick or on leave or had left. This sense of being overworked and undervalued led her to seek a job change within the hospital. She was successful in her application for a care assistant's position in the oncology ward. At one level she feels that moving from the restaurant into this position has changed people's attitudes towards her. As she says, "You get a bit more respect I think, because people, actually when you are walking around, people think you are a nurse. You have to correct them now and tell them 'I'm not a nurse', but you do generally get a bit more respect." And yet, while she finds the work more interesting and rewarding and is not as overworked, she still feels that "Even in the job I do now there is not much appreciation by staff." Her own description as to why this is the case has more to do with the power and hierarchy structures on the ward than it does with her background. "I take a couple of days off and I go in and they say 'Ah! Jesus, it's great to see you back', but that's as far as it will go. ... I don't think that's to do with where I am from, a lot of people wouldn't even know where I am from."

In an odd twist of fate, I was to spend a lot of time in the unit where Michelle works in the hospital, as my daughter was treated there when she was ill. I got to see and to engage with Michelle in her everyday work setting on a number of occasions. She would go from patient to patient as they received chemotherapy, taking away their empty chemo bags, supporting patients with a word or a reassuring touch as they began treatment sessions that would leave most of them feeling ill for days and weeks afterwards. The family of one patient who passed away thanked her personally in an online acknowledgement. She had built up a strong rapport with the person as they had gone through their chemotherapy. She shows me this acknowledgement on her phone one day as we chat in the waiting area. Dressed in a smart hospital uniform, she fills the waste and sharps bins with chemo bags, transfusion bags, used cannulas and reams of plastic tubing that were used during the process. She was conscious of where she was in the work hierarchy and would occasionally refer to staff who would give her orders or instructions to do particular jobs or pieces of work. "She likes to hear the sound of her own voice," she says in passing one day as a senior nurse instructs her to go and do certain tasks. The transition from the restaurant to the ward also carries with it a new emotional labour that has a heavy burden of care, and Michelle's description of the work is imbued with this sense of emotion and profundity.

'It puts life in perspective and you sit and you have a conversation with someone and they are like oh I am going to beat this, and they are so positive. And you wonder where they get the strength from you know, and people moan and I moan, everyone moans about daily stupid things … but the sad thing about it is you know, here I work on the day wards, so when the patient gets really sick with cancer you don't see them. They go to the wards and you just don't see them anymore and you go ah! Jesus. And then you might hear they are after dying or passing away … and you get a bit upset but it's not kind of real, if you get me.' (Michelle)

Allied with the burden of working in the hospital, Michelle has also carried the burden and the hardship of housework and child rearing that went with being a single parent for most of her time as a parent. She has a clear understanding that sex roles are clearly delineated, with women fulfilling caring roles and men occupying a different position in the social hierarchy. As she describes it, "The ideology of a man in Bridgetown is that they are real hard and you have to put on that hard front … it's like a symbol put on them they have to live up to, where with a woman, no, you can just be yourself I suppose." The sexual division of labour that exists in the hospital also filters its way into the sex roles that men and women play around caring for children and housework. As she describes it:

'regardless of where you were from, I think a woman's life would be harder … where your kids are concerned you have to kind of run around, rally round. Housework, probably work yourself … I think that it stems back from years ago and I don't think we are fully out of that yet, where on the whole the man sits back and does nothing. You know don't get me wrong, I do know [some] men that help out an awful lot and probably do more than what a woman would do. In a general aspect I don't think they are equal, they are not on a par. It's still expected of a woman to do all this, not as much as would have been years ago, but still.' (Michelle)

Nadia

'I love living here because you would never be lonely.' (Nadia)

Nadia squatted into the Bridgetown Estate with her partner and child when she was in her late teens. She hadn't grown up on the estate and suffered a little bit of culture shock at the beginning when she arrived:

'I was terrified because I came from a, not that my house was any different to anyone else's, but the quietness when you live on a quiet road. And you come in here and like I was hearing people over me and under me. You wouldn't be used to that noise.' (Nadia)

The marriage wasn't to last long, and the man was gone within a short time. "He said he just didn't want to be married and left," Nadia says matter-of-factly. For a period of time after her separation she received only a small portion of the benefit she was entitled to because most of it was still going to the man who had left, even though she was the one raising the children. She was now a single mother illegally occupying a council flat and expecting a child. Being pregnant saved her in one way, as she says: "We had no rights. But they couldn't evict us because we were heavy pregnant, that was the law." The issue was resolved when the council transferred her with another family, legalising both their tenancies as part of the transfer process. This resolved the issue of someone squatting, Nadia says. She got no extra rooms or space in the transfer going from one one-bedroom flat to another one-bedroom flat. To date she has spent almost 40 years in the same flat and has raised her three children in it. She says that she was never given a transfer to a larger unit because she had ongoing rent arrears when the kids were small. As she says, "You wouldn't get a bigger flat unless you had a clear rent receipt and we never had a clear rent receipt. There was always two or three weeks four weeks, five weeks, and then they would bring you to court." Agreements were reached for a proportion of the arrears to be paid back over time until it was cleared. Such struggles have been a permanent feature of Nadia's life on the estate. She would face many such struggles, and became fiery and resistant in response. She would also develop her own understanding of the common conditions people found themselves in, and an awareness that even in the harshest of times there was a sense of solidarity.

JB: So are people less precious?
Nadia: It's not that they're less precious, it's just a community
            that everyone kind of is in the same problem, if you
            understand me.
JB: Yeah?
Nadia: There's none of them any better than anyone, you know
            we're all equal. Do you know what I mean?
JB: Umm. Really?
Nadia: But you always have a neighbour … John, you can always
            go to your front door and stand, and no matter what day or
            hour it is you'll always see someone passing and say how are
            you or whatever.

Apart from very brief periods after giving birth, Nadia has had an almost uninterrupted paid working history since she was a teenager in various jobs and occupations. As she says herself, "I have worked since I was 17. I was never idle." She is one of a generation of women from the Bridgetown Estate who worked in the clothing trade in one of the many textile factories that were located in the city at the time. Many of these were close to the estate. She had started working in a sewing factory as a clipper when she was in her teens and had graduated to using the cutting machine, and in the end worked on almost all of the different machines in the factory:

> 'It was piece work you know, and kind of how many you get out you do. ... That's the way we worked, and we would all get our bonus at the end of the week, which was Friday. You might get an extra seven pound fifty you know, it doesn't seem a lot, but it did then, John.' (Nadia)

If she had any problems a neighbour from the estate working on an adjacent machine would help and show her how to proceed. She says that she was always good with numbers, but reading was a problem, especially if she was given written instructions as part of a job or a task. Like others, her difficulties with reading are buried deep in her psyche and she talks of being sent to a hospital in the city for treatment when she was a child. Textile factories were places of employment for hundreds if not thousands of people in the city at this time. After the births of her first two children, she was back working within a very short period of time. She could return, she says, because of the support she received from her mother, who minded the kids while she was at work. She lost a lot of blood during the birth of her third child and was seriously ill for a period and couldn't return to the factory. She tells me the sewing factories were dying out, with almost all of them closing within a few years of each other. The end of such a significant industry had a profound effect on the estate, especially on the women who worked in it. This shift to post-industrial or late capitalism, its meaning and the effects it had on a whole generation of people, remains a largely untold story. It exists as memory in the stories of those like Nadia. She went from textiles to the earth, and found work in a mushroom factory, but was made redundant after four years. Within a short period she got a job in a large retailer and enjoyed good conditions. As she says, "I was getting 15 pound an hour and I was working morning shifts and they offered me another contract that meant I would have been working on Saturdays and Sundays, so I said no." When I ask her why she finished, she says, "I worked there for nine years ... but then I got arthritis and I had to come out because of running in and out of the freezers all day." She thinks that sleeping for many years on a sofa beneath the old windows in the sitting room of her flat while the kids had the bed was also a cause of the demise of her health. She says that she would leave towels on the windowsill to prevent draughts and they would be 'wringing wet' in the morning. She thinks that the condensation and moisture penetrating the room also penetrated her body, with serious effects. Her foot is twisted almost at a right angle, and she has been waiting a number of years for an operation to straighten it. She also has a major operation on one of her knees during this period, giving her back some of her lost mobility. Despite being on invalidity benefit, she has sought out and taken jobs on various government-funded community employment schemes. Her desire to work remains undimmed. A friend on the estate acts as a support and brings her to the 'big shops' in her car on a regular basis. Nadia is consciously aware of the importance of such acts of care. In our conversation she describes it as a central characteristic of life on the estate since she arrived. She talks about the older matriarchs in the block who would look out for young parents helping, them out when they could:

> 'The old neighbours like the likes of Mrs G and Mrs H and Mrs N, they were great old women. They would always make sure that you had enough to eat and they would know by looking at you whether you had your money or they would ask you 'have you got potatoes' and all.' (Nadia)

She says that people shared what they had because they found themselves a lot of the time in desperate situations. There were also some altruistic people who helped in this regard, like one of the local shopkeepers who ran a 'tick' system and would offer people credit on a weekly basis with a limit of £20. If the limit was reached, the offer of credit was withdrawn until some payment of the debt was made. This shopkeeper was well known by many people in the estate, and I have heard the story of how important his 'tick' system was for people in distress. For it was usually women who found themselves having to try to find the resources to feed children on a weekly basis, and pooling and sharing whatever they could to put enough food on the table and to make it seem at the same time as if things were still OK. Nadia describes an immense struggle to survive that engendered a sort of potlatch system of collective sharing among women who knew, perhaps, that their children's survival depended on it.

> 'We were all, there was none of us any different. We might have had husbands, some of us hadn't got husbands, we were all in the one boat. None of us had anything, we had no money, we had nothing, and that's the way it was. And everybody was the same, there was no one she was better than her and he was better than her. It probably was, but like they didn't, they weren't getting an honest day's living. They were probably getting it somewhere else, but that was there. But no, everybody that was around you was in the one situation, none of us had anything. And you see if you stick with one another in here we help one another, do you know what I mean, like I often went up and Helen would have a sack of potatoes, I would have a tray of eggs and Bernie would have loads of beans and sausages. And there was the

kids's dinner. I would give her potatoes, she would give me eggs, she would give me beans, and that's the way it was.' (Nadia)

This desire for a good life for one's children is a perennial theme, and Nadia says that her children have done OK and have all got good jobs. She says similar things about her own birth family, saying they were all 'well educated', with some of them running their own businesses and sisters in good jobs "in solicitors' offices an' all". She has some sort of expectation that her children will reproduce the lives and conditions of her own brothers and sisters. And even though all of her children are working, they have not been spared the austerity of recent years. I have spoken to her son on a number of occasions, who tells me how he paid 'mad money' for a house in County Wexford, only to see the whole thing collapse with the crash in 2008. For much of the intervening ten years work was scarce and he could pay interest only on the mortgage and the house price had completely collapsed. After almost ten years he managed to sell the house for much less than he paid for it, and, after a period living back in his mother's flat with his own child, he has recently bought a small two-up, two-down terraced house in an old Dublin working class-estate. He says that he still has a lot of debt from the first house, and he is starting from scratch again, but he feels that he has sorted one part of the problem. When he was younger Nadia was worried that he might take the wrong path, and fought ferociously to keep him away from the darker side of life on the estate.

On a summer's evening in 2019 I meet Nadia and her friend Mandy as they sit in Mandy's car, chatting. Mandy has taken Nadia to one of the larger shopping centres on the edge of the city to do some shopping. Friends for many years, they are in reflective mood as warm air permeates the estate and lots of people are sitting out and walking. They talk about how things have changed on the estate over the years. They are worried about what they see as new patterns of violence and a lack of respect from young people on the estate. The part of the estate that both of them are living in is due to be demolished soon and Nadia should have moved already. But her thorny relationship with the council has persisted into the present. Hoping for what she considers a good outcome for herself, she is deeply unhappy with what she has been offered and now remains in the abandoned block along with a handful of other residents awaiting a resolution. Her block has become curiously silent now, with almost all of the people living around her gone as part of the transition to the new housing on the estate. In a strange reversal of sorts, she yearns for the intensity of the noise and frenetic activity that unsettled her when she first arrived.

5

The food chain

'There is no poverty today. You will never starve. You can dress
your kids in Penneys for a few euros. There are loads of places
you can go. There is 'the Brothers' [religious organisation] where
you can get a breakfast and then you get the takeaway bag with
bread and rashers and sausages and with a pint of milk and butter
and some soup. They give you your breakfast and then give you
your dinner a few times a week. You mightn't be able to go out
for a drink an' all but you will never starve.' (Carmella)

The trip to the religious house is but one of a series of events and practices
that take place in particular locations at particular times over the course of a
normal week. Children are dropped off at the creche. Groceries, cigarettes
and alcohol are bought in local stores. There are visits to the post office
to collect a welfare payment and to pay rent and where tea is also taken
in the adjoining café on the odd occasion. There are visits to community
projects where specialised supports and cooked meals are provided. There
are hospital visits and clinic appointments. Lunchtime venues are attended
by some. There are unscripted, spontaneous rambles throughout the local
neighbourhood. The block is the base to the entire superstructure, in that
everything starts and finishes here. The block functions as the roots of the
tree, as it were. These events or activities constitute a micro-world and a
particular style of life and are defined to a large extent by a set of particular
material conditions that shape people's lives.

The weekly excursion to the "other place", as Rosy often calls it, normally
begins from Tina's step. The other place signifies a place and a non-place,
in that it simultaneously exists and doesn't exist. That is, that no one or
few people know that Rosy and the others go there. Or if they do, they
don't say it publicly. This goal of the trip mixes together material necessity,
social ritual and habit. There is usually time for a smoke and a chat before
departure, and sometimes tea. Sometimes this takes place inside the flat;
at other times it is on the step outside. The conversation is peppered with
concerns and desires that percolate through the women's lives bridging past,
present and future. These moments are often about daily struggles and making
do from day to day. Resources in a general sense are a constant worry, as is
money and how little of it they have. They talk of the intricate systems of
borrowing that exist among themselves and also what they borrow from
private financial institutions. Rosy borrows €20 from Tina each Thursday

and pays it back, as she says, "religiously the following Monday". Rosy also does the reverse and lends money to other women on occasion. Getting it back can be a problem sometimes. The immediate intermingles with more long-term issues like one's housing situation. Rosy is preoccupied as to whether she will be housed in the new housing when it opens. Things are stricter now than they were in the past, with rent arrears and 'anti-social' being used in a more disciplinary fashion by the city council. She has to fill in a transfer form that has to be stamped in the tax office to ensure that she owns no other assets or property. She laughs at the idea of having assets or property. Tina, who will be part of the first group to move back into the new housing when it opens, has different worries, in that she is receiving letters from Seetec, a government-appointed employment agency, telling her she must attend group sessions for re-employment. Steph sums up her own situation one day when she says, "I used to have money but I have nothin now." She worries about her children and how they are going to manage. Teresa, as a relative newcomer to the estate, has worries about herself and her family settling in. Tina, Steph and Teresa all have adult children who are trying to make their way in the world. Not having enough is constant, whether it is not having the resources for school clothing or books or for Christmas, or the forlorn hope of any sort of a holiday. The people in the group have accepted to some extent this lack for themselves but have a fierce will and desire to ensure that it will not be the fate of their children or grandchildren. Opportunities to supplement one's resources are therefore sought out even if they are frowned upon by others or carry some stigma. Charlie is also part of this loose informal group, but generally makes his way ahead of the others as is his custom. I have become part of it myself for an extended period of time over the years 2017–20.

Each of the women has her own 'buggy'. A buggy is the name given to lightweight children's prams. I have come to understand that the buggy is the workhorse of the dispossessed in that it acts as the crucial piece of carriage equipment in the lives of women who don't own cars. Carrying children is only one of the functions of the buggy. In many ways this is a minor function. There is no little skill in dexterously placing, and travelling with, an inordinate number of objects on every possible part of the frame and also beneath. Their level of day-to-day use is such that the rubber wheels are often worn down to the metal and the buggy is then discarded. They are sometimes 'robbed' from an entrance hall, never to reappear – perhaps underlining their value. Sometimes they do reappear, and someone will say "Ah, I just took it for a little while. I had a few things to do." The buggies and their patrons are the source of a generally unacknowledged but extremely low carbon footprint.

When we set off, we make our way slowly along the long road that passes in front of each of the horseshoe blocks. This offers a quick pick of possible conversations with any number of people and a possibility to see what's happening in each block we pass. This trip is but one fragment of the ineluctable temporal rhythm of the estate, with people setting out on thousands of peripatetic journeys from sun up to sun down. The arc rises with the early morning worker and school runs and falls with those returning from late shifts or parties retiring to bed in the early hours of the morning. There are occasional violent ruptures in this cyclical flow, as when a man is stabbed late at night in his flat over a drugs quarrel or when young men punch the head off a young man in the middle of the day. There is usually a massive wooden fire built and lit on the old football pitch at Halloween. At the end of the long road we pass through the L-shaped block before breaking the threshold of the estate and joining the broader flow of city life. There is an opportunity for Rosy to run to the shop and get some cans of lager and place them in the bottom of the buggy. She will fill a plastic bottle from one of them as is her custom, instead of drinking from the can in public. Sometimes she will put the buggy in front of me and say to me "push that will ya John while I sort this", making me self-conscious. We cross a busy road and are now on a direct route to our destination. We pass valuable old houses and empty derelict factories that are now closed down where Rosy used to sell papers to workers as they finished their day's work. The water hydrant signs, a black capital H painted onto a rectangular yellow background, are always touched for luck by almost everyone as we pass them. They are attached to garden railings and fences along the route. These are totems of sorts, and to touch them is to give oneself some luck. These journeys provide an initial way of getting to know this group of people. There is still some superstition around. I met Steph on one of my first visits to the religious house when she had travelled there with Linda, another woman from Bridgetown. Over time Steph became more and more part of the group with Rosy, Tina and Charlie, and occasionally Carmella, a friend of Rosy's, would come too. Steph had lived on the estate for a number of years and now lives in an adjacent street. Teresa also became part of the group for a period of time after moving into the estate in recent years.

Charlie is normally already there when we arrive. His obsession with being on time means he goes ahead of the group to be first in the queue. His logic is that the time you lose by being early you more than make up for by being first to leave. His practice often undermines his own logic, however, in that he often waits for the others, to return with them. He adheres to a highly structured routine. Much of it is tied to finding economical solutions to living within the limited means at his disposal. He has an intimate knowledge of the useful charitable organisations in the city and uses some of them on a daily basis. He asks me directly, on one of my first visits, "What are you coming here for if you don't want food?" He relaxes then, and so do I. Others in the group often ask me why I am not 'getting a bag' and I say by way of an excuse that I couldn't carry it home on the bike. It seems to mean that if you receive food here you cannot judge or criticise. People often hang around outside and converse. The numbers of people coming generally seem to be growing, and it is usually women with children who make up the largest part of those attending.

Although large, the house is old and unmaintained. The front door opens at the same hour on the same day each week and people must wait outside until allowed entry. There is a waiting room to the left as one enters where people sit and chat when they come in. The waiting room is unkempt, with old plastic chairs, and has some religious statues on the mantel of a tall fireplace and a light-infused reproduction image of Jesus on the wall. There are bundles of second-hand clothing left on a table for those coming to sift through. People are quick to search and to see if they can find anything they deem useful. A batch of used school uniforms is one such deposit. There are sometimes arguments about people who take too much or who 'grab' for the clothes. These arguments can sometimes contain an ethnic or racial tension. There can also be a touch of the absurd, as when there is only one shoe from a pair, for example, which happened one day, leading to a fruitless search for its match that was repeated by every new entrant as they came in, with (variations on) the phrase "That's lovely. Did anyone see the other one?" There is a diverse ethnic make-up each week of Irish people, Irish Travellers, Africans, Asians and Eastern Europeans. The attendance is highly gendered and the majority of those who come are women with children. Some women are accompanied by male partners.

Sometimes there are prayers in the waiting room, but more often they are in a separate, single-storey building at the back that may have once been a large shed but has been converted into a small chapel for residents and visitors alike. This room is clean, with white walls, and some pew seats have been installed. Prayer in the chapel often precedes the distribution of food parcels. On a small blackboard on a wall is a list including duties and prayers to be said for members of the order and also for 'the Holy Father'. The phrase 'Our distribution families' is written at the bottom of the board and refers to the families, like Steph, Rosy, Tina and Teresa, that come each week to receive food. On occasional dates a registration book is produced and names of those present are checked and are ticked off. The walls also have miniature representations of the Stations of the Cross, and at the top of the room is an altar and a life-size statue of the Virgin Mary. Charlie is given the task one day to place flowers on the crown of the statue. In printed letters on the wall behind the altar is the phrase 'I thirst'. The same phrase is also printed on the wall in the room from which the food is distributed. There is an assumption that those present know and understand the rituals and that they will be willing participants. If this tacit understanding were written down or said it would be something like: "If you come here you must believe in God and we expect you to participate in the/our rituals." Those who come into the small church are encouraged to read passages from the Bible or to initiate a Decade of the Rosary or to say the Our Father. Charlie occasionally tries to do this, but says to the rest of us that he gets mixed up sometimes and can't remember what comes next and gets embarrassed and stops. Rosy usually reads these situations and picks up the line if he trails off. She jokes that Charlie "starts in the Hail Marys and ends up in the Our Fathers". Charlie himself says, "I'm OK if there is just one person but if there is more than one person I just lose it." He has talked of how he was sent to a special school when he was young and is still angry that they just left him and didn't do any work with him for a long time. In conversation about school at Tina's step one day he says with deep resentment, "I didn't speak until I was four or five. I didn't speak at all, I had to teach myself to read using the [news] papers and books." Charlie says he still struggles with "all of that stuff" but, as proof of his progress, he buys the *Evening Herald* every day in a paper share with Janet in the block and gives it to her when he is finished. He also gives me a book about the life of young Dubliner called *Wild Child* and tells me he has read it from start to finish and has already started on something new.

Unlike Charlie, Rosy loved school but was expelled after an incident in which she and a group of friends locked themselves in a school classroom after taking the teacher's keys. Her mother didn't chastise her too much and said to her when it happened, "Well, you'll just have to get a job now love." And yet, somewhat ironically, one of the tasks she takes on is to write 'the letters' to the charity organisations such as the St Vincent de Paul for many people in the block who are seeking support. (People are usually given vouchers that can be used to purchase items in the shops or food, if they are successful). She is sought out by people for this task. Tina also struggles with reading and this feeds into the prayers and songs in the chapel as missals that include the Nicene Creed and laminated sheets with hymns such as 'I Kneel to Thee' and 'Christ be my Light' are passed round. As she looks at it, she says to me, "I can't read that". She takes a little comfort and laughs silently behind her laminated sheet at my out-of-place-ness here.

In the chapel and in the waiting room small rites of instruction are passed on. An older religious one day gives a short tutorial on how to bless oneself properly. Verbal commands are given as to what to say when one's hand touches each part of the shoulders, head and chest. The correct words must synchronise with the correct part of the body at the point of touch. The religious watches as people repeat the instruction and then asks people to genuflect toward the statue of Our Lady as they leave the room. On another occasion there is a parable about a shepherd and his flock of sheep. The religious has a small green book in their hand, and on the cover is written the words 'The lost sheep.' A large shoebox of miniature hand-painted figures of shepherd and sheep in a farm setting is produced, and these are laid out in a paddock on a green silk cloth and those present are asked how many sheep are in the pen and are any missing. The religious ask people do they know who the shepherd is, and Rosy turns to the rest of us and asks quietly, "Who is the good shepherd?" Those present are told that no sheep will be left behind and that the shepherd will search and search until he finds a lost sheep. We discover that the shepherd is a stand-in for Jesus, who will seek out those who have strayed from the flock or got lost. The message seems to be that Jesus never gives up on anyone. These events are full of questions such as "Do you know what Pentecost is? Do you know the significance of the month of May? Do you know that it was John who gave Jesus his name? Do you know there are two types of the consecration of the sacred heart and only families can access one type while everyone can access the other? Do you know how the Christian calendar is broken up?" One day we are given a visual lesson on the Christian calendar and how it is broken up throughout the year. This is done using a wooden circular board that is divided up over the course of the calendar year using a colour-coded schema.

When the prayers finish, those present make their way back to the waiting room and the distribution of bags of food begins. Sometimes there are arguments between people as to who is next in the queue. This brought about the introduction of a formal numbering system whereby each person is given a number when they arrive, clearly indicating their place in the queue. The new procedure does little to reduce frustration and has shades of more formal institutions. Those who come are overwhelmingly female and many have children with them. Some come for the food but not for the prayers. They sometimes claim something happened, causing the delay. But there is an expectation of participation in rituals and there is also an implicit set of rules as to when one has become a full member of the congregation, as it were, and receives a full share. On one occasion Janet, who didn't normally travel with the group, turned up but was given a smaller bag of food than the rest and was very unhappy with this. When outside she is angry and says, "I won't be coming back here again … they only gave me a little bag of food and they gave everyone else loads of food." She feels she is a lesser being because she is receiving a lesser share. Carmella has a similar experience on other occasions. The others in the group are quick to support Janet by giving her some of their shares. And yet, they thought she was expecting too much too quickly and reasoned that she hadn't yet 'put her time in' and she didn't have enough 'brownie points' to warrant a full share, as it were. Responding to this incident, Charlie has described how he too only received small amounts when he came first. The day after this incident Rosy asks rhetorically, "What would someone do if they had no money and they needed food badly?" and answers her own question by saying, "The religious are really good because of what they do for people."

Janet reasoned differently and thought that food distribution should be the same for everyone, regardless of how long one had been coming. This issue was also raised on another occasion by Linda when she said that she thought some people got more than others and it wasn't fair. She has the following encounter dialogue with Rosy:

Linda: They have favourites, the religious. Did you see what they gave to your woman? Four of them long bread rolls, bags of donuts and bags of cakes.

Rosy: Maybe it's because she has more kids and if you have more kids you get more food.

Linda: I have the same amount of kids as her and she gets more than I do and so does your man in the blue car get more than I do. What's that all about?

While the debate highlights the acute consciousness that exists as to what is fair and just, the lesson appears to be, however, that the giver has the power to determine who will get what and how much. There is also little knowledge and no input into the rules of the game, as it were. Rosy and Charlie have their own analysis as to how one becomes a legitimate participant and receives the maximum share, as it were. But nothing is said or written down to say that this is actually the case or how it works. But they seem to genuinely believe the distribution is fair and that it is OK for people to have to work their way into the system or up the ladder, as it were. It is also perhaps worth noting that the giver has not produced most of, if not all of, what they are giving. This is something they have received due to their location as a respectable/status-holding player in the field of charity, as it were. This suits those large food retail organisations who drop food here, in that it reduces waste costs while making and advertising such gifts as an altruistic gesture.

Opposite the waiting room is the food store where some of the religious are sorting out the content and size of each food parcel. In order of arrival, each person hands in their bag and waits. The door of the food room is kept closed for most of the time, and the room has a cavernous, treasure-like quality about it. Bags are handed back quickly, and if there is a surplus of bread, of which there often is, people are asked if they want some extra. A lot of the food comes from large food retailers who pass on products that are close to their sell-by date. Their products are identifiable by their unique branding and packaging. The food functions as a capital of sorts in that when it no longer has a direct economic exchange value it then assumes other charity values (perhaps of the gift) as it passes from one set of hands and one mediator to another. As the food passes from large retailers to the religious they then possess it as a slightly degraded but nonetheless valuable resource over which they assume the role of gatekeeper and clearing house. This attracts those in need to come to the house to seek supplementary resources. The offer of food acts as a mediating mechanism for attracting and introducing people to God, and the question arises as to how many people would turn up if there were no food.

Once outside, there is usually a stock-taking of what has been given out and what differences there are in each individual bag. The bags usually contain items such as bread, pasta, sugar, vacuum-packed sliced meats, yoghurts, cheese sticks, vegetables such as carrots or cabbage, biscuits, cakes and chocolate. A lot of the food is high in fat and sugar content. When people are assessing what they have received there are often requests to exchange items between people, or sometimes people make direct requests for certain things from others. When Linda asks Rosy "Give us some of your yoghurts will you?" Rosy tells her, "Get the fuckin boat will ya", and then relents and gives her some. On one occasion Steph comes out and says to all present, "Sure they told me 'we have no yoghurts this week but if you pray they will be here next week'." There is laughter at this. Yoghurts seem low on the list of what one would pray for. At the time of important events in the Christian calendar like Christmas or Easter there is more food distributed than in a normal week. When I ask one day how people came to know about the religious house, Steph says, "A man and a woman came to my door one day and I told them that I used to be grand and have money but now I have nothing." Charlie says that he came first with Rosy because he didn't want to come on his own. Rosy doesn't really remember how she started coming, she says. Rosy and Charlie introduced Teresa, but she also knew others who went. Steph's experience shows that the religious have ways of finding people whom they consider a good fit with their mission and what they do. They visit people in their homes in what seems to be an informal assessment process, and once told Charlie when they visited him that a calendar from a Chinese takeaway that he had hung up had the 'wrong spirits' in it. When she hears Charlie tell this story in her flat one day, Teresa removes a similar calendar from the back of the sitting-room door. A young adult woman who watches her take it down says, "That's just mad, that is."

Some of the food and the clothing that is acquired at the house is shared out back in the block. Food staples such as sugar and bread, or clothing items like school shirts or track suits, are often redistributed to others in the block who need them. As we are leaving the house one day Rosy says, "I don't know why I come here, I just give it all away anyway." And she often does. This redistribution often happens in gatherings around one of the steps in the block after people return. When she received a bag for a friend who couldn't attend, she gave it to someone else saying. "She needs it more than he does now." It is easier for someone like Rosy, who has only one child to reshare, whereas for others like Steph, who has a larger extended family, the need is more pressing. Referring to the practice of sharing out the food, Rosy says to me one day outside the religious house "What comes around goes around. That's the motto I live by." In this instance it seems to mean that if you are good to people that goodwill will come back to you in a sort of goodwill rebound. This phrase is often repeated by members of the group and is part of the common cultural stock or repertoire. It has traction and will surface on a number of other occasions in this book.

6

Means ends

Rosy: I never have any money, I always owe money out, what's the
           story with that?
JB: Maybe it's because you don't have much money?
Rosy: Yeah maybe it is, I just know I never have a shillin.
Rosy: (after a pause) I could write a book, John.

In the space of an hour on Tina's step one day a variety of issues are raised, all related to the theme of the cost of things and money. Steph is just back after a weekend visiting a daughter living in rural Ireland and says, "Everything is expensive down there, there's no Dealz or no Pound shop. Things cost a fortune." Steph had once owned a car in the past and says one day, "Everything just went downhill and I didn't have the money for the tax and insurance anymore. So it [the car] just went." Tina, who is sitting beside her on the step, has three large packets of toilet rolls that she has just bought in the Dealz shop and says, "They are six euros each in the big shop but I got them for four euros each so work that out. That means I got one free." Prompted by this, Rosy shares a story that a sibling has been recently diagnosed with diabetes and Charlie is able to tell her, "If they fill in the pink form that is available in the local chemist they will get all of their diabetes medication free." Charlie and Steph, facing each other across the step, then exchange stories about how many items they have on their 'script' and how much it is costing them and how many they get 'free', as it were. Steph searches her bag and produces a tattered prescription and reads down the list and she and Charlie compare what items they have in common and how much they are spending on them on a monthly basis. Charlie says that he pays for ten items at €2 per item, so his monthly script costs him €20. But he says he also gets eight things 'free' on the script. Steph had told me that there had recently been a reduction in price per item from €2.50 to €2. Entering one particular local chemist to get some of these items is an experience in itself, in that it feels like stepping over a threshold deep into the past. There are huge, oddly shaped jars like giant perfume containers containing vivid-coloured substances, and wood-panelled glass cabinets with exotic names like Matana engraved on brass plates. On another day Cathy, a woman who lives in the block, comes past the step with a supersize box of washing powder and Charlie asks her "How much was that?" "Eleven euro" she responds. "That's about right," he says, "you can get it in Dealz or Mr Centz for that price."

On a freezing cold day just after Christmas, when Steph arrives at the step she says, "There are great bargains to be had in Penneys, jackets for 14 and 17 euros." And yet, it seems that she hasn't bought anything. Rosy takes this cue and pulls up the torn and dirty collar on the jacket she is wearing and says, "I have to get rid of this." She cares about how she looks and what she wears, but her focus and money, like that of others in the group, has shifted from oneself to one's children. She talks nostalgically of buying new Levi jeans when she was younger, when she had paid work, but has not been able to do so for a long time. Now she has little or no money to spend on the care of the self. Rosy is adamant that a child must have two sets of new clothes for Christmas, one for Christmas Day and one for St Stephen's Day. She is irritated by a woman she knows who puts clothes on her child for St Stephen's Day that are not new, thus breaking with what is expected. On ritual occasions like Christmas, social comparisons and competitive pressures of display and possession are intense between families and children. The stoking of (in most cases unrealisable) desire is constant. In a local café with me and Charlie one wet Friday afternoon, as the rain pours down outside, Rosy makes a clear distinction between what she thinks her child needs and what they want. She makes a strong case for prudence against the pressure she feels from others as to what her child should be getting. On another occasion discussion and debate takes place between Rosy and Steph over a couple of days as to where the best 'hair do' is to be had for the best price. Rosy goes into the local hairdresser's and comes out and says "Its 30 [euros] in there." Steph replies by saying, "Ah, no way you can get it cheaper than that." When I meet them the following day Rosy tells me that Steph managed to get her hair done for €15, while she ended up paying €25. Both of them had their eyebrows done together in the same place. Alongside the importance of how oneself or one's children dress or appear to others in public, there are other, more pragmatic, consumption necessities.

Cigarettes and tobacco function both as core commodity and as social lubricant and interconnector at the same time. They are central to the lives of Steph, Tina, Rosy and Teresa in that they all smoke. Although he never drank, Charlie admits that he had only really stopped smoking because of the necessity of surgery for a life- threatening cancer. Speaking about this operation, he says the priest gave him the "last rites" and then corrects himself and says, "No, it was a blessin, it was a blessin he gave me." In the community café one day Rosy is trying to work out how much of her tobacco she can reasonably share with Carmella, a friend of hers who is often in the company. Rosy's cigarettes of choice are the brand Mayfair, but when things are tight, as they usually are, tobacco is a cheaper option. She tells Carmella that she has already given some of her tobacco to Teresa, but she carefully breaks off some more tobacco and gives it to Carmella in a tissue. (Steph had just told Rosy that Teresa didn't have any money to pay for the electricity in the flat, meaning she had no light and no way to cook.) After Carmella leaves, satisfied with what Rosy has given her, Rosy says to me, "Whatever about everything else, you can't do without a smoke." Sorting Carmella was seen as an obligation and not an option. When cigarettes are scarce the second half of a cigarette will often be passed unconsciously from one to another for the next person to finish. In the group, cigarettes are probably the most shared thing between people, other than time. In Teresa's one day, Carmella says, "I was told by a doctor that filtered cigarettes have one thousand toxins but roll-up tobacco only has one hundred." On another day Rosy complains of pains in her lung and says, "I have to stop smoking them dodgy cigarettes." She is referring to cigarettes that are sold on the black market in the estate. Even if the health benefits are thought about, they are subconscious or subliminal most of the time, in that buying tobacco is usually a pragmatic response to the high price of standard filtered cigarettes in the shops. Tina explains to me one day how long a packet of tobacco will last her, but says that it also depends on how much she shares. Not sharing one's cigarettes or tobacco is frowned upon and there are often intense disputes about what is acceptable in this regard. "That's a hungry cunt" is the most regular put-down in this regard, thereby denying any shred of personal identity to the one who is deemed illiberal in the sharing process. In Teresa's flat one day her older child berates her younger sibling severely for not sharing some sweets with Rosy's child. In the same vein Teresa will often lend her bus pass to Rosy if she has no money for the bus fare. Tina tends not to buy standard cigarettes at all and usually buys her tobacco in the post office when she receives her benefit money. She usually buys a magazine or a toy as a treat for Rosy's child as part of this visit. There are occasionally bargains to be had in the block, with packets of tobacco on sale for less than the commercial price. On the step one day Rosy shows me a new packet of tobacco and explains to me that "Britney up there [pointing up to an upper balcony] is selling a 50mg pack for 13 euro and a 30mg pack is normally 12, so that's good value." The opportunity to make a saving and to procure more quantity for less money is very welcome. In an extension of this entrepreneurial spirit, Britney also 'raffles' her car at one point, selling 49 tickets at €20 per ticket. I am told that carefully crafted Christmas hampers, PlayStations and iPhones and, more recently, gins and whiskeys are raffled in a similar fashion. The process all happens online. The price of a raffle ticket varies with the value of the prize, and the winning number is the one that is drawn last in the national lottery draw to avoid any claims of cheating. Hence the rationale for selling 49 tickets, one for each of the lotto numbers. This practice has become more and more prominent through social media networks. As has the practice of raising money for funeral costs through crowdfunding fundraisers online.

Just like tobacco, below-cost (dodgy as Rosy calls them) filtered cigarettes are also on sale in the estate at around €5 for a packet of 20. They have the brand name 'Excellence' on them and have a blue lightning-strike design running down the white box. There are varying views as to the quality of the product. Fergus, whom we often meet as we walk the streets, says to us outside a house on the trunk road one day, "I know all cigarettes kill ya but some of those cheap ones are pure poison." On another occasion myself and Charlie meet Ned as we walk through the estate. He has just been rehired as security guard on a construction site and is making his way to a seller of cut-price cigarettes who is a different woman and a competitor to Britney. Thinking about his purchase, he says to us, "They're poxy. I know. But they're cheaper, so what can you do." Over a period of time I meet more and more people who are buying the cheaper cigarettes on the basis of significant savings and trading the saving off against the 'dangers' of the unbranded cigarettes. There are multiple ironies in the contrast between branded and unbranded cigarettes, perhaps none more so than the distinction between which is more and which is less carcinogenic and whether perhaps there is any difference at all. One has no way of knowing, it seems, which is the greater of the two evils. Rosy also shifts more and more to buying the 'Excellence' brand. Teresa runs up a small debt with the cigarette seller over time, through getting them on tick.

If below-cost cigarettes and tobacco are part of an informal economy within the estate, the large retailers and off-licences retain a monopoly over low-cost alcohol. While all sorts of illegal drugs are readily available in the estate there are, as of yet, no regular sellers of alcohol. But, just as with food, tobacco and other necessities, there is a similar process of economising on alcohol and a constant seeking of the lowest price. On one occasion when I accompany Steph to the local retail outlet when there is a block party taking place, she buys 12 cans of shop-brand alcohol to be shared out among the group. Each can costs an average of 65 cents. As we leave the shop she looks at me and says in unconvincing fashion, "It doesn't taste too bad either." She then bursts out laughing, as if she has to convince herself. As often happens, if one brand of alcohol is cheaper in an off-licence that involves a longer trek than going to the local one, so be it. Rosy asks me, Charlie and Tina one day, "I'm sorry about this lads but it is 50 cents cheaper a can so are yous alright walking?" Like the arcane chemist's shop, the off-licences too are worlds unto themselves. When we are in one of them one day the man working there tells us he is paid just above the minimum wage and that the place has been "robbed loads of times" and says, "I've been here for some of them." When he tells us this Rosy looks at him directly and says sternly, "Just give them the till and don't argue." Robbery of local shops is a regular occurrence, leading to the introduction of self-service machines, and there are almost no cash transactions anymore. Rosy says that Tina's daughter tried to get a job in the off-licence, but they said they only employed men. Increasing the strength of the beer seems to be a priority. Some of the beers in the off-licence have high alcohol content, such as the one that is branded as 8.6 (8.6% alcohol). 8.6 generally costs €3.50 per can, but there is one off-licence that sells it at a bargain €3 per can. Carmella says of the 8.6, "It takes the lining of your stomach." Jack makes much the same criticism. "Stick to the Coors," he says. On another day Rosy shows me the recently introduced Amsterdam Maximator can of beer that has an alcohol content of 11.4%, which she says she has only ever tried once. As we look into the richly stocked polished-glass fridges, Rosy and myself discuss why beer needs to be so strong. Picking up on this cue, the man behind the counter boasts of the Maximator, with not a little pride, "Yeah, that's the new one now", as if he had made it himself with great effort. The off-licences and beer stores are an integral part of the local economic and cultural infrastructure and there are more of them appearing, it seems. The local off-licence on the trunk road in Bridgetown is one part of a large commercial chain. One of the simple reasons for seeking the cheapest price is that it is very rare for people in the group to go for a drink in a pub because they simply cannot afford to. They rarely if ever go to a restaurant either. Like a mini stock market, the prices of products and comparisons of prices filter through conversations in the estate all the time. Just like they share almost all information about possibilities in the charity and community sectors, people share information about bargains and options in the shops.

People often look for loans or credit when they need or desire things that their incomes cannot provide. I first hear about the 'loan man' in the block one afternoon when Rosy tells me about this man who "comes around every Friday for his money", and she tells me, "He works for a company who lend people money in the estate." He generally arrives at the same time every Friday afternoon and rings her phone, and then she feels that she can't avoid him. It is in the block that I get my first glimpse of him. He is young, of muscular build, with a tight-fitting shirt, and drives a large, powerful saloon car. His physical strength appears to me as a deterrent if someone is thinking about stealing the money he collects. I hear many stories about the 'insurance men' who in the past used to collect premiums on the estate being robbed. For a period of time, Tina, Charlie and Rosy and a number of others in the block and the estate have loans with the loan man. Rosy names around ten people off the top of her head one day when I ask how many people have loans with him. This is just in one specific block in the estate. When I ask Charlie one day what the loan from the loan man was for, he says that "I bought a washing machine and a cooker out if it." When I ask him why he didn't do it through 'Electric Ireland', he says "I thought that was the best way to do it." Rosy says that she had no other credit available to her. I then ask Charlie what the loan man charges and he says, "Thirty in the hundred." He clarifies this and says "for every 100 euros you borrow you have to pay back 130, so if you get 300 you have to pay back three [hundred and] ninety." Charlie puts his own household economy in a concise summary form when he says, "When I pay me rent and everything I owe, bills and all, I might have 40 euros left to do me for the week." He has this precisely allocated to expenses, like the two euros he pays for his main meal each day, six days a week, in a charity café in the city. One day we meet Harry, who is 'tappin' (begging) at the local shops. Charlie is frustrated and turns to me and says "I get 193 [euros] a week and that's all I have to pay me rent, me food and me bills, so if they think I have money to give to them they can fuck off." And yet, on another occasion, at the funeral of a man who worked in the community café, he puts five euros in the collection plate. And when I go with him to the charity café for a lunch meal, he insists on paying for mine.

Referring to the loan man, Rosy says that "Some people just stopped paying him", and that as far as she is aware there was no comeback or implications for the people who stopped paying. "I just couldn't do that. In any case he'd find me in the block or wouldn't stop ringin me phone," she says. Charlie says that when he missed one payment, he got a letter from the company saying his credit rating was at risk. The last time he seeks a loan off the loan man he is not successful and says that he has told him that he must be a tenant in his own right and not just 'on the rent', as he shares the flat with a sibling who is the official tenant. It is news to me that only tenants can access credit from him. The chances of Charlie disappearing if he is tied to his own flat are less. One sunny afternoon when a group of us are sitting around Finn's step, Rosy has €30 wrapped tightly in a bundle in her hand and asks out loud, "Will I pay him this week? It's Father's day on Sunday and I need to get something for him," referring to the father of her child. She is a combination of giddiness and guilt at the decision facing her and decides not to pay him this time. What seems like easy credit at the beginning becomes difficult to pay back, and repayments are a significant portion of weekly income. Tina, Rosy and Charlie eventually manage to finish their loans with him and begin to use the local credit union instead. "What the fuck he charges thirty in the hundred where in the credit union it's nothin like that," Rosy says as she begins to realise the cost of the credit. Nonetheless, it has taken Rosy a while to change credit providers and look for cheaper credit. Charlie tells me one day that there is a new scheme being advertised for people in credit unions with what he considers good loan terms. One of the attractions of the loan man, it seems, is his proximity and the ease with which money can be accessed on the spur of the moment. He will come directly to you in the block, and he deals with people in a very informal and friendly manner and after some brief checks the money is offered very quickly. Loans are tied to important rituals. The biggest ritual and expense for Rosy and for Tina and others is Christmas. One day in the community café Rosy responds to a question about how much Christmas costs by saying that she spent €1,700 on stuff for her child and on Christmas overall. "I borrowed a grand from the credit union," she says. If she can just about manage Christmas through borrowing, Rosy is upset by the fact that she has not got the financial wherewithal to take her child on holiday. This lack intrudes deeply into her sense of her obligations as a parent. She feels this one day when a neighbour says to her that the other kids were away for a week when hers "only got red sauce and chips" at the religious house. She laughs it off, but it cuts.

As well as formal credit institutions there are also informal loan and credit systems of giving and returning that operate between people within the group and beyond. This system is perhaps far larger than the formal finance and loan systems. Rosy has a regular arrangement with Tina each Monday that sees her borrow money from her and then pay it back a few days later when she gets paid. Rosy will lend money to Steph or other people if they ask. Steph has given a large loan to a friend in the estate and is struggling to retrieve it. Herself and Tina have also lent money to another woman and are both awaiting its return. Steph is also constantly trying to support her own children in various ways with money and time. This sometimes extends into helping with their debt. If one of the group is stuck for money, as often happens, other people will try to help out. On one occasion when Teresa had no money for electricity or gas or food and was a few days shy of her benefit, Rosy "got a lend of a tenner" from Benny, a friend, and then got a loan from Charlie the following day to repay Benny quickly and then, when Teresa repaid her two days later, Rosy repaid Charlie. When I ask Rosy why Benny would lend her money that she was going to give to someone she says, "Sure it's my money now so I can do what the fuck I like with it." Rosy felt that the real problem was that Teresa's children were asking for too much money for things like phone credit and smokes. There are also other people beyond the immediate group who will lend money to people on the understanding that it will be returned within a relatively short period, and the cycle starts again. When we return from a summer project trip one day Rosy hands Meg, a neighbour of Tina's, €20 in through the kitchen window and says to me, "I am paying my debts while I still have money." I become part of this informal credit system, giving people a fiver or a tenner occasionally, and the same rules are strictly adhered to in that it is always returned and never seen as a non-reciprocal gift. Rosy or Charlie will pay my lotto if I am not around or have no money. I am often given chocolate by Rosy as well as the money returned, and on another occasion the group produce a birthday cake and chocolate for me at Liz's step. Rosy often builds linguistic analogies between my taste for chocolate and a heroin addiction with phrases like "Are you dyin sick today John?" "I heard there's a drought on, what are you goin to do?" "You're goin to be in bits if you don't score soon won't ya?" These impromptu comedic routines give the rest of the group a laugh and are what Freud called innocuous jokes.

The lotto offers a cosmically long-odds hope of fixing and resolving all financial issues, and there is a web of different lotto groups that weave through the group and the block. As we leave the estate one day Rosy expresses with confidence, "Sure if I win the lotto I will buy me own house." (When she sees the city council restoring a house close to the estate one day we all go in and have a look round and she says, "I would like to live here, especially when the child gets older.") After a period of time with the group I am asked if I want to join the EuroMillions lotto syndicate and I agree to do so. I have to pay €2 each Friday, along with nine other people in the block. As well as the EuroMillions some of the group also do the Irish lotto, and some also do the 'three number lotto' in the bookie's, for shorter odds but with a higher chance of winning. If the three numbers you pick are among the winning numbers in the national lottery you win €750. Or 'seven fiddy' as Rosy often says. Charlie manages the lotto fund and pays it every week and lets people know if there are occasional small wins. (There are €50 of small wins in the kitty at one point.) He also asks for advice if someone hasn't paid for a number of weeks and acts as if they are still in the syndicate. Would they get money if there is a win is an important question. "Fuck that, if they haven't paid for five or six weeks, they're out," Rosy says. Rosy does the Irish lotto separately along with Tina's next-door neighbours Jim and Meg, and they rotate the payment week on, week off. Charlie has a similar arrangement with Janet to 'do a lotto' each week. If he has any spare money Charlie also does the 'Lucky 15' accumulator bet in the local bookie's once or twice a week. The bet costs €3 and I often go with him to the local bookmaker's to check the board for winners, which are rare. The shop has events feeding in from all over the world on multiple screens that fill one entire wall. The effect of the information feed is wildly disorienting. Charlie wins €6.50 on one occasion and when he comes out with the money in his hand Rosy says, taking the piss a little bit, "That's exactly how much Harry needs for a q." She is laughing when she says this, and Harry is sitting outside the local shop, begging, with a column of brass coins in his hand but says he is still short six fifty for a q (of heroin), as it happens. Charlie told me that he had once won £3,000 when he worked in the bookie's when he was young and was afraid that some of the people who frequented the booking shop would try and rob him, but some of the other punters made sure he got home OK. "I gave them a few bob for looking after me," he says. The lotto is a relatively small gamble and seems to function more as a social ritual and action in that it keeps contact between people and commitments must be maintained. There are other people in the block who play serious bingo for big money prizes that takes place in large venues. Alice and Britney often go, and it costs €40 for a night. On one occasion Alice tells me she won €1,000 playing this bingo game, and on another occasion €200.

Rosy has many bags of worn children's clothes in her flat that she wants to bring to one of the shops that give you cash for clothes. She asks Jim will he give her a lift, and he agrees. Jim, Rosy and myself make the trip. We travel out of the estate and Jim makes a short stop to check a bet and then at his place of work to check to see what jobs he has on in the next few days. In the block he often talks about the different jobs he has been doing; he has a lifetime of experience in construction and glazing. The work is intermittent and stop–start. One week might be a full week, he tells me, and then it might be three days a week for the next two or three weeks. As we head towards our destination on the outskirts of the city, he tells us a joke about a man who is chatting up a woman in a bar and tells her that he has the name of his home town tattooed on his "you know what". As he tells it, "So what's the name of your home town?" the woman asks. The man responds, "Newtownmountkennedy." There is a pause before Rosy asks, "How big were them letters?" The joke is followed by Rosy talking about the stories in the *Sunday World* newspaper about 'the gangs'. We arrive at our destination and carry in the bags of clothes from the car. The place is an old shop and there are bags stacked on top of each other three to four high and deep all along the wall on the right-hand side. To the left there is a small bookcase with some books, including John Green's *The Fault in Our Stars*, and there are also two volumes of a work entitled *A History of the Tobacco Industry in Goa*. I admire the author's dedication to their subject matter. A tall woman comes and begins to open and go through Rosy's bags of clothes and is muttering about the nature of the clothing, and Jim and myself go outside for a minute where he lights up a smoke. Rosy comes out exasperated and says, "She's a cunt." She pauses, and then says more slowly and with more venom, "She – is – some – cunt." We go back in, and the woman is nearing the end of the bags and says that she cannot do the last two or three, appearing to have made up her mind that the clothing is not of a high-enough quality. There are four or five of the bags still sitting on the floor and Rosy says "Fuck that, I am not leaving them here. She is not getting them. The way she talked about the clothes. What does she expect when you have kids, of course their clothes are going to get worn. It's just the way she picked them up and looked at them." In the end the woman hands Rosy €16 for the clothes and a receipt. Rosy is in a foul mood as we leave the shop and I say that I have had a similar experience in a clothing shop where I live. Rosy is still seething over the nature of the interaction and the way she was treated in the whole affair. When we get back to the block all of the remaining bags are thrown into the large communal waste bin. Teresa comes into the block as Rosy is putting the last of the bags in the bin. When Rosy tells her of the experience in the clothes place Teresa says "I got 30 euro for my stuff up there the other day." Rosy looks at me and smiles wryly when she hears this.

7

What goes around comes around

As Steph is rummaging through the clothes on a table in the religious house one day she picks up a T-shirt with the words printed on it 'Happiness can be found even in the darkest of times if one only remembers to turn on the light'. The words are inlaid into a white and green floral print that is set off against the black background colour of the T-shirt. Steph is taken by the line and reads it aloud before she measures the T- shirt up to the front of her body, showing it to the rest of us. The following brief dialogue takes place.

JB: Is it true?
Steph: It is.
JB: Is it true all the time?
Rosy: Ah well, that's a different story.
Teresa: But it's a nice poem all the same.

This chapter explores two particular myths and beliefs that are expressed by people in the group and the realities that in turn confront these. It is also about what people say and do when faced with harsh realities. People in the group use such phrases, perhaps one could even call them myths, and tell them to each other (usually unconsciously) to make sense of events and even to provide a particular logic for such events. The phrase 'what goes around comes around' is redolent of ideas of virtue, morality and justice. It has a 'you get what you deserve in life' element, but it also refers to the idea that there is some process of reciprocal justice (natural/divine) that inexorably works itself out in the world. The second phrase, 'it's not where you live but how you live that matters', appeared earlier in Michelle's story and has a different logic and applies more to place and to the attempt to transcend the limits of place and to the idea that one can do this and live a dignified life as long one knows how. Whatever problems that exist in or are attached to a place can somehow be transcended by living in a virtuous way. And yet there is an acknowledgement that one may have to leave the estate to lead or to try to find a good life. There is a connection between the two, in that both phrases are grounded in the ethicality of life in a public housing estate and what is acceptable and what is not, and the struggles and emotional attachments and commitments that people have to living lives free of scarcity, violence and contempt.

What goes around comes around

In the block one day I learn that Teresa's daughter has been jumped on by a group of young people on a recent evening outside one of the local shops in Bridgetown. The fallout from this event continues for a period of time. A few days after the event Rosy, Steph, Teresa and myself are in Teresa's flat, and she is talking about the effects it has had on her and her family. Enraged and deflated at what has happened, Teresa is thinking about leaving the estate. "It's Bridgetown. I hate it here," she says. Rosy responds to this in a protective manner by saying, "It's not the estate Teresa", implying that one must make a distinction between people and place or between good and bad people, or that the place doesn't somehow make people bad through a process of osmosis. As people are getting tea and lighting up smokes, Rosy, sitting on the sofa, says the phrase "What goes around comes around", referring to the people who jumped on Teresa's daughter. Although it is a well-worn phrase I am puzzled by its use and try to explore its meaning as it arises in this natural setting and ask clumsily "If you are born into a family with no money does what comes around goes around hold good and do you get what you deserve?" Rosy responds initially to the material part and says, "Yeah, that's my family you are describing," but then she shifts to the do you get what you deserve part of the question and says, "If you do good to people, people will do good to you. But if you do bad to people it will come back to you. You were put on this earth to …" Rosy's flow is interrupted by Teresa, who pulls up her sleeve, revealing text on her arm. "Sure I have them words tattooed there on my arm," she says. The phrase " what goes around comes around" is tattooed in small, flowing script on the soft tissue of her upper arm. She had shown this to us previously, outside the religious house one day. When she saw this tattoo script Rosy said, "That's the motto I live by." A few days later, when we are sitting in the community café, someone has blurry footage on their phone of Teresa's son having what Charlie calls a 'straightener' (a fight) with one of the young men who had jumped on his sister. The two men in the film go back and forward, trading punches with each other. Teresa says she can't watch it, but I wonder if she is still proud of her son for defending the family. When Rosy sees it, she says, "Fair play to him."

Another incident occurs when one man stabs another, younger man in a dispute over drugs. This happens outside one of the hallways in the estate. As I catch up with Steph, Rosy and Carmella not too long after on the main road they are discussing what happened. They are shocked by the violence of the incident. When I ask what it was over Rosy tells me, "It's all over the crack [cocaine], John. It's all over the crack." They tell me that although the injuries weren't life threatening, the man wielding the blade stabbed the man a number of times, breaking the shaft of the short blade, and even after that he stabbed him a few more times before desisting. The stabs seem to be superficial and deliberately strategic and not aimed at vital organs. (I was told later by people that the reason for this type of below-waist attack was that it was underpinned by a preordained knowledge that stabbing someone above the waist carried a much longer jail term.) They then tell me that he then bullied the other man into telling the police when they arrived that the two of them had been jumped on by another group of men who had then fled. Carmella says, "That youngfella is some woman's son. That's not on." Steph says, "It's a bad thing to do something like that to someone else." Rosy finishes the turn and says, "If he did that to my child I don't know what I would do." Not long after this, as we re-enter the estate we meet the man in question, and when we do, Rosy challenges him and asks him "For fuck sake – what did you do that for?" Still high and in a state of defiant giddiness, he says, "I just needed to stab somebody." When he is gone Steph says, "Did you hear him trying to justify that, for fuck's sake?" Carmella, who is clearly angry at what happened, says, "If I couldn't get him from the front, I would get him from behind." The story still has legs at Clare's step two days later and there is still a sense of raw anger at what happened. When Rosy arrives at the step, she tells us that the man who stabbed the other man went over the handlebars of his bicycle earlier in the day. Rosy describes a scene of him cycling along before hitting a pothole and crashing head first over the bicycle handlebars onto the ground. She says that her child had said to him innocently, "you need to use your two hands —". When she hears Rosy describe the man falling off his bike, Clare says with a smile, "Karma's a cunt, isn't it", to the rest of us. There is a little bit of cosmic retribution in this unfortunate accident, it seems, or perhaps a desire for it. It is not lost on me that Clare, Rosy, Steph, Tina and Teresa are mothers, and are heavily invested in the safety and protection of their children. In congruence with this view, Rosy had said on a previous occasion at the step, "There is two things I hate. One is robbing handbags and the other is robbed cars." It is perhaps no accident that one involves violence against women and the other involves direct risks to children and people on the estate.

On a different day at Clare's step there is talk of the drug dealing that goes on in the estate and how these issues are affecting people. Rosy says matter-of-factly, "Some of them are doing well out of it." Clare and Lara respond to this and say almost simultaneously, "I would never want to live like that, looking over your shoulder all the time." There is a pause for a few moments and Clare continues and says, "I would rather beg on the street and have nothing than get involved in that stuff." Rosy withdraws her comment and accepts the position of Clare and Lara, not wanting to draw out the difference between morality and truth. "I was only sayin," she says. A few days later we are at Finn's step and Janet has a 'Spot the Ball' card with the names of 16 football teams on it that she is selling as a fundraiser for the local dance group. True to her vocation as gifted fundraiser, Rosy goes door to door and sells all of the teams that are left. She uses the pitch line "every little helps" as she sells the last of the teams. A man on one of the upper balconies across the block wins and Rosy goes to give the man his prize of €20. When the game is over the conversation shifts to the new housing that is being built and when people will get to see it, and Janet says, "Sure all the drugs will be moving over as well." I ask her "What's that all about?" and she replies, "Sure every second person is selling in Bridgetown now." Not sure how true this is, I ask why there is so much dealing in the estate and Jack says, "People need to put shoes on their kids' feet John, that's the way it is." Janet feeds off this and says, "If you see someone on social welfare coming in with new runners and all that you have to ask where all that came from." Jack tells Finn that he has been off the drugs for six years now but that it took him 30 odd years to get to that point. "Fair play to you, Jack," Finn says. When the group breaks up and I am walking away I understand Jack to mean that people sell drugs for the most pragmatic and rational of reasons. I also wonder about questions of demand and supply and the scale and density of the drugs market in and around the estate.

On another day I accompany Rosy on a trip to the clinic. She is searching for Teresa to borrow her bus pass but has no luck and we make up the bus fare between us and walk to the main road. As we wait for the bus a man Rosy knows, driving a high-spec chauffeur taxi, stops beside us and says hello. Dressed smartly in pressed slacks and shirt and tie, he says he has a job on and can't give us a lift. Rosy "buzzes off him" as she says, and tells me she knows him from when she was younger. He tells us that he has his own house and is "doing well" before driving off. When he is gone Rosy says. "Fuck that, he could have given us a lift," and then as a wistful afterthought says, "He is right not to come back." Minutes later as we continue to wait for the bus a woman is passing whom Rosy knows. The woman slows down and they say hello to each other. Rosy tells the woman about the very recent death of someone who had been known to be involved in drug dealing in the area many years ago. "Did you hear about —? He was buried yesterday." The woman seems to have prior knowledge of this event, having heard about it already. She stops in her tracks and turns to face us and, without any hesitation, says with some force, "All the people they put in Mount Jerome. What goes around comes around." The woman walks off. When she is out of earshot Rosy tells me a story about a relation of this woman's being murdered many years ago, and Rosy thinks that she has good reason to be angry. Rosy tries to recall the exact details of what happened. The woman's pain is clearly still raw after many years. There are many stories like hers that lie scattered around the place, waiting for an opportune moment like this to find a release even if it is momentary and unsatisfactory.

Another of them arises when I come to the block on a fresh spring day. Rosy and Steph are sitting on the step outside Tina's flat. Rosy says that she has been on the radio this morning. Surprised, I ask her what it was about and she tells me that they were talking about a woman who had been seriously assaulted. She says that she had sat and listened for a while to the radio show and, as she describes it, she became more and more agitated at what was being said about the assault. She says, "Yer man battered that woman over in —. You know who I mean John." As I get my bearings I sit on the step, and she continues, "I sent in a text saying you are right [DJ] he was only a dirty pox for what he did to that woman." Charlie joins us at the step, having made his way across the block from Finn's flat. Rosy continues and says, "I got a phone call then asking me would I go on and I did. And I said it on air that he was a dirtbag for what he did … when he threw her down the stairs and then told the kids that their mammy had just fallen down the stairs." There is a pause when some of what happened over the weekend is discussed and Charlie and myself roll some of Steph's tobacco into roll-ups. "That's a Joy [Mountjoy prison] roll up," Rosy says when she sees Charlie's attempt. After making a plastic helicopter toy from a magazine purchased by Tina for Rosy's child and floating it off the balcony, we leave the block and walk toward the main road. As we do, Steph and Charlie both raise the issue again of the assault and the man who was convicted and say that prior to this assault he had been done for a previous assault on a different woman. When we get near the bookie's I ask Rosy why she went on the radio. She answers me and says, "You just can't have that, John, what he did to that woman it was terrible. The bastard, he left her in an awful state. The DJ was saying there was a bloke who wanted to come on and defend him [defend the convicted man] and he wouldn't let him on because no one could defend what he did. So I just said fuck it and I went on." As she goes into the sweet shop she says to me, "You can get it on a podcast." I am still stunned at her willingness to just pick up the phone without any hesitation or media training and go on the radio to make her case against violence against women.

Whatever remaining distance is offered by radio collapses when I hear that Steph has been sexually assaulted one evening, leaving a local social club. I first hear of the assault from Charlie and Rosy at the performance of a play we all attend. When we chat outside at the half-time interval, they tell me she was assaulted the previous night but neither of them has spoken to her yet. The next morning, I meet Rosy and her friend Linda as they are waiting at a bus stop. When Rosy tells Linda what happened, Linda is livid and says, "We should go round to his gaff, the little cunt, and once a woman says she doesn't want you to touch her you shouldn't touch her and that's the end of it." Rosy talks of the bruising left on Steph's body afterwards and Linda says, "That's not just touchin someone when you leave marks like that." Rosy and myself visit Steph at home later on the same day and she describes what happened:

'I was at the club and I had four monster [bingo] cards and I couldn't mark them all myself so I gave one to someone else and then this other group came over and joined us and I knew them to see. Me other half was gone off with the darts team somewhere else. Then around 11 I was leaving and this man said sure we'll give you a lift home and then he said that he would drop me down first and come back for the others and I went around the other side of the car and it was like a child lock and then he came after me and grabbed me there and then down there and he had me trousers half way down and I ran back inside and said he is trying to rape me and I heard someone say that's not the first time he did that.' (Steph)

When we leave the house Rosy comments on how shaken Steph looks from what happened. There is initially a flurry of police activity and at one point Steph says that they are going to charge the man in question, but when I ask her months later as we walk along the main road Steph says that she has "heard nothing from the old bill for ages now".

Doogy is a phantom character who has the ability to appear and disappear in a moment. One minute there is nothing, and then suddenly he is standing beside people at the step. He induces tension in people as soon as he arrives somewhere and there are many stories of his unpredictability and violence. At the step one day someone says he is in the block somewhere. Someone else says that he just jumped in beside a woman in her car yesterday in the block and told her to drive him somewhere. The police arrive in the block, apparently looking for him, and stop for a moment at the step. They search unsuccessfully for him, and when they leave he appears, asking if anyone had told them where he was. Janet says fearlessly, "No one rang the old bill, Doogy." He says, "Ah, Janet, I was just checkin." Soon after Rosy appears out of Tina's flat with her hair in a towel and we leave for the religious house. On the way she tells me stories of his unpredictability and how he once tried to rob a bike from inside her old family flat, saying he just wanted a lend of it. "You have to stand up to him John," she says. I ask how he can keep doing mad stuff and getting away with it and she says, "What goes around comes around John." When I ask is that really true and ask, "Did the people who ran the banks really get what comes around?" without thinking too much she replies to me, "Ah, it's not really the same is it. They didn't hurt people like him. Did they?" Charlie had said to me of Doogy on another day, "People do say that if you ever cross with him, you'd have to kill him because he would come back so you'd have to kill him."

It's not where you live, it's how you live

'I am from Block A, so I'll be going back there.' (Rosy)

On the bus into town one day Rosy tells me about being in rent arrears after her mother died when they lived in the old family flat, and trying to sort it out. After a period of time they managed to sort it through a payment plan between herself and some of her siblings. Money was deducted from people's wages and benefits weekly, until the arrears were paid. Later herself and two of her siblings were rehoused in their own individual flats. She got a one-bedroom flat that she says was hugely important to her in getting her own sense of independence, and she has lived there with her child for the past few years. She felt that if she didn't get her own place she would become a de facto mother figure and be left with all of the work that entailed. There was an assumption that she would do the cooking and the cleaning. Independence was therefore also independence from the demands of other family members. When she tells me that her child is now officially 'on the rent' I suggest that this might be good in the long term, in that it will give them some sort of a foothold in the housing system. This doesn't seem to give her any sense of reassurance, and after a pause of a few seconds she says:

> 'I don't want them in the estate when they are 15 or 16. I know *it's not where you live but how you live* that is what matters, but the young ones in the flats are wagons and even though loads of them are not from the estate I don't know whether I'd want my child in there or not.' (Rosy; emphasis added)

A similar theme comes up again on a bitterly cold day just after Christmas when we are sitting at Tina's step, eating chips and sausage that are left over from a children's party above us. Afterwards we walk through the estate looking at the new construction as it is taking shape. As we look on Charlie says that the way some of the new building has been done there will be places where young people are going to be able to "hang around and get up to no good". As we stand there, Lara, whose flat overlooks the construction, comes out and says that she wants to get herself and her daughter and granddaughter sorted as they are currently living with her in her overcrowded flat. Rosy wonders out loud who her neighbours will be if she ever gets a new flat. She is obsessed with the new housing and what sort of a place she will get and when. Lara, who has just taken in her washing, says that her current flat is "full of damp", and that still she doesn't want to move off the estate. "I want to stay here," she says. Rosy responds to Lara and says,

'I never want to leave the area, at least not until — is 12 or 13, and then I will think about it then. All the drugs and all the scumbags and all that. I can control them now when they are at this age but what am I going to do when they are 12 or 13 and I have no control over them then?' (Rosy)

She turns to Lara and asks her, "What about your daughter won't it be the same for her?"Lara ignores the deeper question, wanting to stay in the present. She responds by saying, "I just want a one-bed for me and a two-bed for me daughter." We say good luck and walk out the gate, and as we are going out Rosy says, "Sure if I win the lotto I will buy me own house." On another day when Rosy is talking to a woman who has been given a new council house in an estate a distance away, I ask Rosy if she too would like 'a house' and she says, "Not now John. I am from the estate. I will think about it when my child is older." When she says this, I wonder how she would survive without the support networks she has around her if she left. This was the message she gave to Maxine when she was leaving the estate.

On another occasion at Tina's step there is a discussion about a documentary shown on TV and narrated by a woman about her long struggle with drugs and addiction. Rosy, Steph and myself are present. Steph is sorting some poor-quality clothes she was given that still have tags on them and she is asking Rosy do people want them. As Rosy looks through them with no real interest, she says that the woman making the film "was very, very good on the telly last night in the programme". Rosy had previously raised the issue of the changing tone of the woman's accent, as if it wasn't authentic working class anymore and she had perhaps betrayed her roots by changing her accent. She has an acute antenna for accent change, especially with people who once spoke a certain way and who now speak with a different accent. It signals someone wanting to put some distance between them and their original sound, and therefore between them and her. The documentary is dissected for credibility and the different parts are discussed, including one part where the woman telling her story talks to children about being asked by drug dealers to do stuff for them. Steph says, "The kids were asked to keep sketch [watch out] for the old bill." Rosy takes some of the clothes that Steph had brought down and takes them up to Janet's flat and then comes back down. We make our way out of the estate, and at the entrance gate Rosy turns to me, clearly still thinking about the documentary, and says in delayed fashion, "Anyway it's not where you live, it's how you live." When I hear this, I stop and ask the two of them, "What does that mean?" Steph quickly says, "It means that people talk about Bridgetown all the time and you don't get things because of that." Rosy follows Steph and says, "But it's not just the place." She pauses for a moment and says, "It's your family as well. Even if I did go on the gear [heroin] an all." I follow this up and ask,

"What does that say about the risks around here?" and Rosy says, "The risks were very high when I was growin up." I think this undermines the how you live thesis, but I don't say anything. Steph focuses on the where and the view that perceptions matter and have the effect of blocking or stopping things happening or being given. She has a raised consciousness of the place and the prejudice directed against people from the estate and the ensuing effects. Rosy's logic is different in that she appeals to the solidarity and support of "your family an all". This is the case, even if she did ultimately "go on the gear" as she says, acknowledging the risks. In Rosy's logic, family and friendship networks are a counterweight that have the capacity to deflect the slings and arrows and cushion against harsh blows. Rosy often speaks of her mother as an enormous presence in this regard, and says out of the blue one day to another woman of her [Rosy's] mother that "She was only one woman, but what a woman she was." She tells a group of us at the step one day that her mother used to say to her, "Give me a robber any day instead of a liar." When I ask her what it means she says, "A liar is worse than a robber, John." On another day she makes the statement, "A liar needs a good memory." Steph has similar regard for her father and says she worshipped the ground he walked on. The two of them are expressing the struggle between love and care and the reality of material and perceptual inequalities.

People's relation to the estate arises at Finn's step one day in a different guise. Finn is sitting on his step in casual jeans and pullover and soft slippers and is talking about his life working as a 'coal man', which he started when he was around 12 years of age, and says, "Some days we would deliver ten tons of coal and the sweat would be comin' off me like Christy Moore [Irish folk singer] and the jocks would be stuck to me. I would have to go back four to five times to reload the lorry to cover everyone." Sharon, a neighbour who lives above Finn, comes by and says hello and goes up the stairs and then reappears a few minutes later, joining a group of us at the step. I learn that she only moved into the estate in recent years. Finn is saying that he stopped drinking many years ago, as the drink was affecting his brain, recalling his youthful days when he wouldn't arrive home until three or four in the morning, and says his father would have him out the door an hour or two later to start a day's work on the horse and cart regardless. In those days he says, "fights were sorted out with fists and it's not like it is today with all the guns around". Finn is the last remaining member of his family now inhabiting the old family flat. He names the class–specific places that all of his siblings have gone to over the years, to inner and outer suburbs of the city. Looking around the block with his tea in one hand a smoke in the other he reams off the names of the original resident families of the block we sit in and says that only a handful now remain. "The A's were in that flat there. The B's were in that flat there. The C's in that one. But there's only a few of the old ones left now." He says this with a cigarette burning between his fingers. Almost as an afterthought he says, "Mary Harney [former government minister] ruined the coal business because she introduced smokeless coal into the Irish market."

Sharon asks Finn will he smoke some leaf tobacco that she has brought. She says that a customer in the hotel where she works bought it in error, thinking the packet contained conventional filtered cigarettes. Charlie and myself begin rolling some of the tobacco into cigarettes, and Sharon talks about working long shifts in the hotel and says of the owners, "They wouldn't even give you a drink if you were after working a 15-hour shift." She continues and says, "They are so mean they wouldn't buy their children proper shoes, leading to serious foot problems for the kids." It takes her about 35 minutes to cycle each way, she says. She says that when she came to live here in the estate with her partner she hated it, and wanted to get out as soon as she could. She had grown up in a house with plenty of room and she found the flats small. But over time, she says, she came to like living in the estate. She says that her sister was living in private rented accommodation, which was sold, and she is now back in her mother's house and can't find anywhere affordable to rent. The housing precarity her sister finds herself in is not lost on her. "We are really lucky to live here," she says. Rosy arrives back from the market and puts her bags down. Sharon continues and says, "I would never leave here now. I love the estate." Her partner arrives, covered in dust after finishing a shift working on a site in the city, and stands at the step with the rest of us. He says he is employed through a recruitment agency and that he is almost a foreman on the job now and the boss trusts him, but he says he would like to work closer to the estate to save him the travelling. When someone asks her about the length of time it is going to take before the regeneration will reach this block, Sharon says, "I don't care, we just have to get on with it."

Conclusion

Buried in the phrase 'It's not where you live but how you live' are two interconnected realities. There is a tension between the *where* and the *how* of living, as it were. That which is problematic in the 'where' of place can be overcome by the 'how' of living. One can do this, it seems, by living an ethical and honourable life, a virtuous life perhaps. Families can show you how to do this. Through proper behaviour and comportment one can show the world that one is worthy of respect and deserves respectability and can rise above the violence and the hardship, somehow. Perhaps the most important person to be convinced in this is oneself. One can overcome or transcend the obstacles and the struggles that one encounters and perhaps stay in the place to which one is deeply attached. There also seems to be the possibility of thwarting the negative perceptions of outsiders who have the power and the means to pass judgement by living a 'good life'. This expresses a general desire for a dignified way of life that one feels is OK. But weighted against this are the darker possibilities as to the likelihood of what may happen. The risks of problem drug use and the spectre of violence cast a long shadow and unsettle people. Rosy knows how it works and the dangers involved, which perhaps makes it all the more real and palpable for her. This is not ambivalence but, rather, a profound emotional struggle, for it is the life of her child that she is thinking about. And yet Rosy, like so many others, is profoundly attached to Bridgetown and I have heard her say on many occasions, "I am from Bridgetown. I am from here. Why would I go anywhere else?"

A final 'what comes around'

We go to the clinic and Rosy fulfils her daily appointment as I wait outside. We see Dee as we wait for the bus on our way back. Rosy is shouting at her to hurry up because the bus is coming fast around the corner. She just makes it onto the bus and is perspiring and out of breath. As the bus moves off she begins to tell a story without any prompting of how, a few years ago, she did a robbery with a group of people and got a long sentence for it. "We had done a few of them but this time I had a bad feeling and me ma said whenever you have a bad feeling about something don't do it, but I went ahead and the driver hadn't a clue and we got caught." As an afterthought she says to Rosy, "I was young and stupid then." Without pause Rosy says back to her, "Now you're just stupid." The three of us laugh and Dee continues the story and tells us of doing time with the 'Black widow'. She says about her, "She was sound, she was. She'd come up every morning all done up when I couldn't get me shit together you know." We get off the bus, and after Dee has gone Rosy says to me, "She is a mad thing." A few weeks later in the block Rosy comes and says to me, "Do you know what happened, John?" I ask her, "What?" She tells me, "Dee died." Rosy says she doesn't know what happened exactly, but attributes some of the cause of her death to a drug that she was being prescribed. Rosy has a theory that this drug has all sorts of problematic consequences for people. She connects this drug with the deaths of several people who attend the clinic. She also says that Dee was quite ill anyway and had serious underlying health issues that were causing her problems stemming from her addiction over many years.

8

Fragile beings

Carmella to Rosy at the step one day: The past is history. The future
is a mystery. Live for today.

Rosy: Everyone has a past, John.

(Excessive) fragility is a theme that runs throughout this work. This chapter
further tries to develop and extend this theme that was raised by people
like Frank and Nadia in earlier chapters. This chapter raises questions about
the nature of being-in-the-world for Tina, Charlie, Rosy and Steph. Their
psychological and social selves are the product of events and practices that
have taken place in time, as it were. In their practices and life histories and
life events we learn a lot about how their bodies and hearts and minds
change and diminish over time. The effects or outcomes of such change also
include their own self-perceptions and the actions taken to follow through
on such perceptions. One expression of this was the prominence of disability
as a theme on many occasions in daily conversation and argument. To get
'on disability' was a practical necessity sought by Tina and that had already
been achieved by Charlie and, in a slightly different vein, by Steph. But,
for specific reasons, in the past Rosy had rejected it as a category that she
would apply to herself or a 'good' that she would seek. Central, therefore, to
this chapter are changes in and to the physical body and its breaking down
due to things such as age, the effects of work, illness or addiction. Dramatic
changes can happen relatively quickly to the body, where one goes from
a position of being a relatively autonomous individual to one where one's
physical capacities are diminished within a short period of time. Brute luck
can play an important role in this in terms of the capacities or talents or
physical or mental powers that one is born with or not born with. There are
also chance events that happen, as with Steph when she was burned seriously
in a fire. But Steph, Charlie, Rosy and Tina are also sentient emotional
beings, in that the physical body has an emotional psychic core, and this
dialectic between the two is crucial. Fragility is embedded in the sensuous
and comprehending core of being that animates skin and bone. All of this
takes place through time. There is what has gone before, what is now and
what is to come. So, in this chapter I try to connect the pasts of Charlie,
Rosy, Steph and Tina to where they are now and where they are going.

As we walk into the estate one day Tina tells me that she has received
a letter from Seetec, an employment agency, saying that she must attend
a course in one of their offices in town. She says that "It is for computer

training and all that stuff." And then says, "They won't pay me if I don't go so I am going to go," underlining the obligatory nature of the correspondence. Rosy seems to know about it already and scoffs at this, saying that Tina should be on disability and that she can't read and write. Tina reacts to this and says to her, "What are you saying that for? You shouldn't be saying things out of school like that," displaying something of her sensitivity to the subject. Rosy is chastened a bit and backs down when Tina challenges her. This subject of whether Tina should be on disability or not comes up on many occasions over a period of time and it seems that Rosy is arguing that it is in Tina's best interests to be on disability because of problems with her physical health, and perhaps because she is unlikely ever to do paid work, due to her lack of skills and capacity. As I understand it, Rosy sees it as a legitimate and necessary claim.

Tina has mobility issues and is slow walking and struggles to keep up with the others. She also has difficulties climbing stairs and has difficulty standing freely. Rosy repeats her view after Tina has a visit to the doctor for an assessment and says it again as we sit in the community café one afternoon. When she does, Charlie and myself ask if there are any potential benefits in doing the course, such as the possibility of Tina improving her literacy. Rosy is deeply sceptical and has no faith that the course can deal with Tina's issues. As she sees it, it is more about getting Tina off the unemployment register than dealing with the issue in any profound way. Rosy's logic seems to be that disability is the best option for Tina because she cannot participate in conventional employment situations, due to her lack of literacy skills and debilitating physical issues. If Tina is on disability, she will no longer get letters from Seetec because she will be removed from the normal unemployment register. At Finn's step a few weeks later, after she has been to one of her first group sessions, I ask Tina about the course, and she says that she has been doing some literacy so far. She then says that she never went to secondary school after finishing primary school, and that she cannot read long words and remembers that her teacher in school told her to break up long words into small sections in order to be able to read them. Her literacy struggles pop up in places like the religious house, where she looks at me and laughs when the prayer books are handed out. When one of the religious asks people to read the Our Lady from the prayer sheet one day, it makes obvious those who can read and those who can't. One day when she has moved into her new flat, she writes out column after column of maths sums in a small copy book as we sit around a table. She gets embarrassed when Rosy and myself ask her why she does them and closes the copy.

Letters or forms that come in the post, like the one from Seetec, cause other problems, and Tina often asks Rosy or other people to help her with these. She trusts Rosy more than most, even though they argue a good deal. They have been friends and neighbours for a long time. Despite many attempts, it is difficult to work out the substance of Tina's life, as she doesn't speak that much or have a life narrative as such. I have spent almost entire afternoons in her company with the others without her saying anything. I know a good deal about the life she leads in the present, but the past is blurry and lacks the normal chronological signposts by which people track the evolutionary stages of their lives. After a period of time, Rosy writes and lodges an application for disability for Tina, but within weeks she gets a rejection letter in the post. When Charlie hears this at the step he says, "I had to apply a good few times before I got it, so just apply again. Don't let that stop you." I think this is more a sign of Charlie's signalling his own success and persistence than it has to do with empathy with Tina. Rosy builds a bridge from Tina's individual predicament to a broader one of people who, as she says, "were on the gear [heroin] back in the day" and who were then put on methadone and were automatically offered the option of going on 'the disability' at a certain point in time. She says that this happened to many people she knew, and she says a lot of them took the option and have been on disability since then. Many of them have also since died, she adds. She lists the benefits and possible attractions of disability as the 'free travel', 'free television licence', 'fuel allowance benefits' and 'electricity allowance'. (Perhaps because none of the group have a car, 'disabled parking' doesn't enter into her thoughts.) Therefore, if you are on disability, you get some extra benefits that you do not get on standard unemployment benefit. Charlie points out that you have to be a tenant in your own right to get some of them, such as the free TV licence. Rosy talks about them in a way that stresses how critical such resources are for people when resources are scarce. But, after listing these other benefits that she thinks might help Tina, Rosy says that it wasn't for her and says, "I wasn't disabled, so why would I go on disability. Fuck that. I was workin and then signin on and that was enough for me." Despite the benefits, it seems she didn't want the hassle, nor the designation, nor did she see herself in that way. It is often Rosy who will address issues that develop for Tina, whether it be letters or communications issues with state agencies or the council. She cares about her and what happens to her, even if she frustrates her on occasion. She is also the unofficial letter writer to charitable organisations for supports within the group and for a number of others who ask her.

These questions of one's changing relation to the world over time are important for Rosy, Tina, Charlie, Steph and Teresa. Tina's application brings to light the fact that this subject of 'dis-ability' is in fact knitted into the fabric of the group in various ways, and is related to how lives change through and over time. There are many questions about what it even means. It is really only by viewing their lives over time that this emerges. It must be conceived as something more than purely physical, as the issues that filter through the group connect both the body and the mind. Tina's issues and those of others in the group reach beyond the physical and into the soft tissue of comprehension and understanding. Their bodies and minds carry a class geology of sorts that was laid down in layers over time and continues into the present and beyond. Those related to the mind and the intellect reach back into childhood for all of the group, and have followed them throughout their entire lives.

Since his illness, Charlie has been on 'disability' and has a number of complicating health problems that need ongoing treatment one of which is chronic diabetes. Steph is on 'invalidity', which carries a slightly different designation than disability. This was after a house fire that left her with significant burns to her body and months in a hospital burns unit. She has also recently had a heart monitor fitted. Rosy has a different set of constraints in that she is tied into clinic visits for methadone every morning, and sometimes on weekends. This regime places limits on what she can do, as she has to collect her child not long after her return. She rages and worries in equal measure at her own addiction, both past and present, and the multiple dis-abling effects it is having and has had on her life. She says constantly that she wants to give up the drink and complains that she is on far too much methadone and doesn't understand why they won't reduce her dose. She wants to be free but hasn't got there yet, despite numerous attempts. And yet, despite all of this the group remains highly active and its members continue to do significant amounts of (mainly unpaid) work, whether it is walking the city streets chasing up charity food sources, playing key caring roles for children and grandchildren or doing various jobs for other, sometimes housebound people, like running errands. Charlie's act of bringing Finn a pre-made dinner almost every day or Rosy sharing out the food from the religious with others in the block are but two examples.

In the community café one afternoon, I get a broader sense of the trajectory of Charlie's life over a longer period of time, when he speaks at length of his earlier life and of leaving Ireland to go to London on his own when he was a teenager. The story unfolds as we eat food and drink tea served to us by Patricia, who runs the kitchen. His mother had died when he was young. He was already working in his early teens in a local market, cleaning and setting out stall tables and doing odd jobs as his schooling faded out. He was also 'doing the board' in a local betting office, putting up the horse names and odds (and a way of filling the deficit in his own literacy and numeracy training) and doing some manual labouring jobs where he learned some plastering skills. When he was 15 or 16, he got a ferry to Holyhead and made his way to London via Birmingham. He describes a rough start to his time in England.

'I ended up sleeping in a park in Peckham when I got there and one night a few blokes tried to give it to me. I was fighting with them and this black woman saved me and she took me in and let me sleep on the sofa and then she got me a job on a construction site with a friend of hers, another black man, and after that I ended up working on sites all over London.' (Charlie)

He says that he "worked on trenches and all sorts of jobs all over London". He reflects on his physical strength and masculinity at this stage of his life, saying, "I could lift anything at that stage. I could have lifted two men, one in each arm no problem. And then I had got a start on the London underground but me owl fella got sick so I had to come home and I just never went back." I have seen at first hand Charlie's obsessiveness with doing things and tasks on time that occasionally frustrates others in the group, and I sometimes wonder if he is afraid that without tight structure his life will disintegrate. Upon returning to Ireland after the death of his father Charlie picked up his father's old job in the antique furniture removal business. He describes work in which skill and care were needed: "There were only a few people who knew how to move antique furniture properly and I was one of them." He mentions with pride one particular job on a stately home on the outskirts of the city for which the Irish government had bought back a lot of antique furniture pieces that had been sold off previously to the US, and his job was to coordinate moving it back upon its return. There were also many long journeys, travelling throughout much of Europe at this time with the work. Without ever mentioning it before, he tells me one day that he spent a period of time working in Toulouse in southern France. He says that he thinks that a lot of his poor diet began when he was doing jobs abroad, as he was literally eating while travelling. He is still very much addicted to sugar and sweets, even though he has to inject himself a number of times each day with insulin. Over a period of time, however, he describes a gradual decline in his own conditions of work and treatment. As he describes it, this began with the arrival of labour from abroad and his being marginalised within the firm into more part-time casual employment. In his words, "the Poles and others started doing the jobs for less and putting in lower quotes and then they put down the wages by 20 or 30 euros a week and they still expected me to carry the responsibilities of being a foreman." His hours were reduced as he was downgraded from full time to part time and, he says, "In the end I just jacked it in."

After he spent some time on a community employment scheme learning the new skill of energy insulation, Charlie's health began to deteriorate in recent years. He was diagnosed with serious illness that required a number of operations and he now needs ongoing continuous health assessment and frequent visits to clinics. Within a relatively short period of time he has gone from a position of relative autonomy to a new and altered state. The physical changes and struggles are obvious, in that his legs occasionally give out from underneath him as he walks or tries to run for a bus. The realm of actions and things he could once do is contracting, but he retains a stubborn will to carry on and his desire to do things and to be active is undimmed. The struggle between his diminishing physical powers and his will to live a full life is most clearly visible in his daily timetable of tasks and exercise. In recent years he has developed a set of strategies and practices in order to adapt to his changed situation. A great deal of his time is spent trying to manage his physical health as best he can. Parallel to this, he seeks out and harvests whatever resources are available to him in the charity and community sectors to supplement the resources he receives from the state. There is a strict timetable of things to do and actions to be followed through each week. All of these practices take significant work and time in and of themselves. When we are outside the local shops one day he tells me that he was listening to a piece on the radio about the numbers of people who are now on disability in Ireland. He says that it was probably easier to get on it in the past than it is now, and says that the people on the radio said that "the numbers have doubled in the last ten years."

Rosy says that she began smoking heroin to come down from ecstasy she had taken after the raves that she went to with all of her mates back in the 1990s. "I loved the what do you call it, the ritual of the foil and preparing it, I loved all that. It was just a lovely way to come down from all the madness, it was." There are also darker stories she tells, of people overdosing in front of her and turning blue, and her anxiety that they might die there and then, and of people on crack carrying dead babies inside themselves. She tells me a story one day about a man putting his hand inside a woman's vagina on the main road to steal heroin from her that she had concealed there so it wouldn't be stolen. She often asks out loud the counterfactual question of what might have happened to her if she hadn't grown up on the estate, and would she have started using heroin if she hadn't. Gigs and music were big in her life at the time, and she tells me about talking to Paul Heaton from the Beautiful South as she walked down the main street in Thurles at 'Feile' in the 1990s. She has other gig stories, like being picked from the crowd one day at a large gig in Dublin to dance on stage with the star. She shows me footage of this event on her phone on one occasion. One day, in Charlie's, she talks at length about what happened at this time in her life and how herself and others were introduced to heroin and the economy that grew up around the drug and how this filtered into her peer group. Her use of heroin, and more lately alcohol as a replacement, is one part of a life that also includes her long back story of paid employment and her becoming a parent in recent years.

Rosy's history of paid work in a variety of different jobs goes far back into her youth and I gradually get a sense of it as she tells it in bits and pieces in various places over time. Before departing on a day trip to Knock with the religious one Sunday morning I sit in the seat behind her on the bus, and her memory is roused as she looks across at the old factory and tells me this is where she used to sell papers with other members of the family as a team. She says that they would time their arrival to catch the workers just as they finished their day shift. Looking out the bus window at the desolate factories that were once humming with machines and activity she says,

> 'See there John [pointing to the factory gate], we would arrive into the factory at closing time when people would be leaving so fast that you had to catch them quick, they would just drop the money and grab the paper and be gone in seconds … there was loads of money to be made in them days and great tips as well. We used to do the pubs of a Saturday night and we sold papers outside the church on a Sunday and we also bought a paper round up around – which included the church which was a great spot for selling the papers. It faded out because people stopped buying the papers, and especially with social media and all that.' (Rosy)

She adds more layers to this on another occasion, saying, "we were out in all weathers seven days a week selling papers and chasing up money from people who hadn't paid their bills", and says that she "got a pound a week" for her endeavours. When I ask her how old she was when she started, she says "around ten or eleven I think". She explains to me that a small number of families in the Bridgetown Estate "done the papers" for many years, but today there are just one or two people that still manage to eke out a living from this business. Rosy tells me that the paper round was sold when newspaper sales began to decline. She took her sales skills into many other jobs, working for everyone from shopkeepers to clothiers to street traders, one of whom told her, "You are my best seller", to which she replied, "Sure it's easier to talk to men than to women." While working in a clothing cleaner's shop she says that she once had tried on Robbie Williams' suit, which had been left in, and on another day a wedding dress, just to see what it felt like. "It didn't really fit," she says.

While Rosy's introduction to the routines of work started when she was very young, it didn't distract her from school, and she says she "loved school" and loved learning. But she was suspended from secondary school when herself and her friends were messing around and took the keys to the school office one day and locked themselves in until the principal arrived with a master key and opened the door. She took the brunt of the blame and says that her mother didn't go to the school to try to sort it, and after this she "just never went back". (Knowing her extraordinary capacity with language, there is something profoundly sad about this.) There was an agreement with her mother that if she didn't go back to school she would go to "the FAS" more formally known as 'Youthreach', a government-run training scheme for young people. It was through this that she got some of her first work experience in the factory of a well-known Dublin fashion designer. "He used to throw us a few quid for doin the work," she says. After finishing in Youthreach herself and a friend walked off the street into a small printing factory not too far from Bridgetown, and both of them got work straight away. Rosy says that her friend wasn't that interested, but the owner trained Rosy on some of the printing machines, and also asked her to do longer shifts stretching into the evening, telling her she could earn extra money. She describes vividly the frightening speed and the noise of the machines. But when she compared her pay with that of her friend who wasn't doing the late shifts, she realised that she wasn't being paid very much extra at all. Her mother came to the factory and argued this out with the boss until Rosy got the money she was owed. "He thought we were just young ones and could get away with it, but I got almost another 100 pound from him, but I never went back." While telling this story she says, "I always gave me ma half me wages." She often makes this point about the necessity of children contributing as soon as they can with their wages. The importance of helping out financially is never lost on her and she is irate when she sees young people earning a wage and not handing up money to parents.

Rosy became a parent herself for the first time in recent years at a relatively late age. Her relation to the world changed with this event, in that she has a relationship of care to her child that she didn't have previously. Her love for her child is unbounded in thought and in practice, and she says one day, in an otherworldly sense, "I think they were sent to me." I am not sure if she means that her child has saved her from herself. On another occasion, "You have to tell them you love them, you just have to." She has tried to maintain a relationship with the child's father, who lives somewhere else, but he has shown no real interest. Of her wish for the relationship, she says, "I would have liked to have been married to — but it didn't happen, so that's it." She is to all intents and purposes parenting the child on her own with support from her family and from friends like Tina, Steph and Meg. Apart from a brief period in the morning when her child is in the creche, she has the child all of the time. "That's the deal you make," she says to me when I ask her about being a parent. Virtually everywhere we go, Rosy has her young child in a buggy or in her arms or holding his hand. There is rarely a moment when she is not caring for them. She discusses how this has changed her life one day when herself, me and Jean are sitting on the step outside Tina's flat. Rosy goes in and makes tea and returns and hands me a new mug with a "Thanks fuck very much" slogan printed on the enamel. Describing her own current bind, Rosy says: 'I always worked and I would love to go back to work, but what can I do when the child is in the creche from half nine to half twelve and I have to collect him, how could you work in that time … there are people who leave their kids in the creche from nine to five even if they are not working … I would never do that.'

One commitment that Rosy must fulfil every weekday is to go to the clinic for methadone. I have often gone with her and there is usually a busy trade of tablets for sale outside as she goes in. It is a mini theatre of the absurd outside the treatment clinic. She must appear in person each day to be breathalysed and appear before the lead doctor on a regular basis. If the alcohol level in her blood is over the set limit, there are a set of ever-hardening rules that come into play, the first of which stipulates that she must come to the clinic on Saturday and Sunday. If breaches of the limits persist, her dosage of methadone will be reduced to half, and if there is deemed to be a serious breach people are issued with a 'Do Not Dispense', or as Rosy calls it, a 'DND'. This means you must attend a meeting with doctors and there is a possibility that you may receive no methadone. She says that if she ever got a DND it would probably drive her back to heroin. The system is designed to make sure that her risks are minimised by disciplining and acting on the overconsumption of alcohol. She often says, "drink is lethal with methadone". Rosy is ambivalent about the regime and describes the workings of the clinic from the time she enters until the time she leaves. She talks of many meetings with the lead doctor, who, she says, lectures her about her life and what she needs to do. She describes these meetings in minute detail, down to where she is supposed to sit and how many trainee student doctors in white coats are in the room and the tone that is used. This head doctor has something of an authoritarian mythology that circulates about her among those who go to the clinic, and in the field of addiction generally. Rosy describes a typical encounter with the doctor when she is trying to secure a weekend takeaway of methadone. "It's up to you to stop drinking Rosy, that's why you have to come in here on the weekend." Rosy says:

'I was shakin in front of her. She rang down to the person who gives her the info and as she was talking to him she was waving her finger at me saying "no no no you blew 52 last Sunday and you want a takeaway?" "I was at a party," I said. In the end she gave me a takeaway for Sunday but not for Saturday.' (Rosy)

The clinic has in recent years become a focal part of her life in that she must, along with hundreds of others, attend almost every day. Trying to stop is a recurrent theme. As she says to me one day, "I was on less when I went in there and they put me back up to 85mls. I want to get off the clinic altogether." On another day she says to me, "I have to blow into the meter down there every morning and I have only ever been over it once or twice, but even so, I want to try and do something." Rosy is acutely aware of the effects that her continued alcohol use is having on her body. In the block one day as we stand in out of the rain Rosy and Carmella have a conversation about the damage that alcohol does to the liver. The two of them exchange concerns with Carmella, wondering out loud. "I'm interested in what happens to the liver with the drinking an all." And then she asks to no one in particular: "But what does happen to the liver?" In a lamenting voice she says, "But I don't want to die Rosy." Both of them have had prolonged periods when they were drug free and then started using again. Rosy says to Carmella during this conversation, "The only good thing was that we never used needles." Both of them have said to me before that they feel this probably saved them from life-ending infection. Rosy is deeply conscious of the effects on both inner and outer body. She often makes reference to her recently distended stomach and she feels it when people make reference to her in this vein. She tells me one Friday, when she has come back from the clinic, that she has been given a takeway without question because it's the weekend of the pope's visit to Ireland. "What do you make of that? Ah, it's OK, you can OD [overdose], the pope is here, it'll all be sorted. Miracles all round. What the fuck?" The two of us burst out laughing.

This theme of fragility of mind and body also permeates Steph's life. Steph was seriously injured in a fire. Although her face was spared, she says she has little physical sensation in the parts of her body that were burned and she has to be careful when taking a bath lest the water is too hot, because she has lost a lot of her nerve endings and won't feel it. She spent a long time hospitalised. In Tina's flat one day, when the conversation is deep on the subject of disability, Steph says that she is on invalidity and this is slightly different to disability, and she is on this because of the burns. As we leave the flat to go to the religious house soon after, she says to me, "I wouldn't be able to work now with the issues I have with me health now." She has regular hospital appointments to follow up. Like Rosy and Charlie, she had had a variety of different jobs when she was younger, mainly in factories. One in particular she says was well paid and had very good conditions. She had told me some of this on the first occasion I met her, outside the religious house on a warm summer's day. Without prompting she tells me about working in a food farm factory where "the money was great" and where she made many female friends and where she describes a strong camaraderie among the workers. She also worked "in the States as an au pair" for a period of time, and the story is full of the freedom and optimism of youth. Her eyes light up as she recalls the memories and the time. Steph met her partner, who already had children, and they subsequently had a number of children together. Some of her children now have their own children and she plays an important role in helping her children and grandchildren to manage. When I ask her one day as to how she found out about the religious house, she says that "someone knocked on me door out of the blue". When they asked her how things were going she says, "I told them I used to be grand

and have money but now I have nothing." Losing the small car she had, because she could no longer afford the tax and insurance, is one of her own indicators as to how life was changing. "I couldn't bring me young one to training anymore because it was too far on the bus," she says. Despite all of these constraints and ills, she is constantly on the move, seeking out supports and resources wherever she can find them. Body and soul have to be kept together somehow.

In the community café at a packed event late in 2019 to launch some artwork done by a group she is in along with Rosy, Charlie and Tina, Steph leads a rendition of the song 'I will survive'. Rosy, Charlie, Tina and myself are there sitting at the circular tables. The song builds slowly, and in a room full of people the place is electrified with the atmosphere that is generated. It takes everyone out of the mundane and forges a solidarity and fellow feeling among all present. For a few brief moments all is forgotten.

9

The word

On Meg's step one day

| Rosy to Carmella: | You are a good talker. If you listen to others they can't do that, but you are good at it. |
| Carmella: | I come from a family like that where people talked. |

Jed is a man who lives on the trunk road, and when the weather is good he sits outside the front of his house behind a little railing watching life go by. Rosy has gotten to know him over years, and she stops to chat with him on our daily route as we pass the house. His health is not good, and Rosy says that he is not looking after himself as he should. In the block one day Rosy discovers that he has died and after getting the funeral details on RIP. ie, Charlie, Rosy and myself attend the funeral mass a few days later in a city centre church. The church is one of the more opulent in the city and sits almost concealed among the wealth and high-end branded consumption stores that surround it. Charlie sits away from us near the door, as he says he has things to do and must leave before the end. Rosy looks at the people around her and says almost to herself, "There are lots of nice people here today." She repeats the same phrase again a few moments later. She is out of her locale and feels a difference between herself and other the people in the church. She will later say to Steph, "They were all wealthy at the funeral." The priest talks about Jed's life and then tells a story about Jesus and informs the assembled congregation, "Do you know that Jesus had a nickname?" No one answers or is expected to answer. Those present are a bit puzzled. He provides the answer from the altar and says, "His nickname was 'The Word'." After the service we leave the church and head to get the bus back to Bridgetown in the pouring rain.

The word has its own existence in the profane day-to-day life in the Bridgetown Estate. The discursive rhythm and texture that infuses and animates the lives of the people in the group is an important theme in its own right. Language is substance, in that it has potency in both its presence and its absence. Whether we are sitting at the step, rambling throughout the area, in the community café or on the way to the religious house, words loom large. The key form is perhaps that of the story. Stories are everywhere. They are about small things and big things. They cover the entire human emotional register, from love to terror and from affection to physical and sexual abuse. They are the spoken currency and verbal economy of the estate. There are stories of the past, of events in the present or what might happen in the near future. The flow of time outruns the stories, but traces remain in their recalling and retelling. Everyone has them, everyone tells them, everyone knows at least some, even the usually taciturn Tina. Some stories have deep emotional anchors that tie people to the living and the dead, while others are the product of mundane, everyday events in a life personal or collective. There are also jokes, puns, myths and even occasional debates on the merits and demerits of abortion. Stories in daily newspapers such as the *Evening Herald* add grist to the linguistic mill. Within the objectivity of the social structure is a flesh-and-blood emotional discursive outflow where struggles for expression and understanding take place. The underside of the presence of words and stories is the lack or void that exists where there is silence and/or struggle with and for words. There is a continuous attempt to remedy such lack, as in Charlie's or Tina's personal attempts to overcome reading and writing difficulties and in the more general flow and banter of daily communication.

Rosy is a repository and cacophony of words and phrases and stories and one-liners that have been transmitted to her in the past with which she pollinates the lives of those she comes into contact with. She has an ear to receive the word and a tongue to deliver. Perhaps the words from the papers she sold as a child were imbibed through some process of osmosis. By and large, they didn't come from the formal educational establishment. She has no formal educational qualifications. In the religious house one day a visiting priest is giving a mass and talks about Adam and Eve and Rosy is quick to say, "It could be Adam and Steve, Father. Or it could be Eve and Eve." He takes it in good spirit. In the block on another day, when I am complaining of back pain, she says, "I once had a lumbar puncture in my vertebrae", and then says to me, "Have you got your fare to Bray, John?" As she writes her child's name on the whiteboard in the community project one day she says to me, "I am a doodler, John, what can I say." She also writes the child's name in wet cement on the pavement outside when we leave. She has an interest in words and corrects her child, saying things like "It's not 'cos'. Its 'be-cause'." Or, "It's not 'member'. It's 're-member'." When Charlie says that bats are nocturnal, after a visit to caves in Kilkenny, Rosy says, "That's a nice word; nocturnal." At Tina's step one day she says that she was listening to the radio and someone rang in and said, "I thrun some pineapple on the pizza", and they were corrected by the radio show host, who replied, "You can say put but not thrun." She is engaged by the debate as she says to me, "You can't be saying thrun now, can you?" Rosy says that she went to elocution and drama lessons in school and tells me a rhyme she learned that goes "This, That, These, and Those, That is how the Th goes." Given the normal dropping of the 'h' by people in the estate and in the broader Dublin working class this stress on enunciation is new and surprising to me. Oddly enough, I also hear one of the regulars at the religious house teaching and reinforcing this rhyme with his children one day. And yet it seems that the lesson hasn't really stuck or got traction. The 'th' has never caught on. One afternoon in Charlie's flat Rosy gives Charlie, Steph and me an unbroken spoken narrative account of the nature of drug use and drug markets at a certain point in time in the estate's history. It is a history lesson about her generation and peer group and about life in the city. Over the course of an hour, she mesmerises us with an account that includes a substantial number of characters who all play various roles in the drama. One of the central characters in her story, speaking to his son's future, had said, "Sure, why would you want to read when all you need to know is how to count?" "What the fuck was that all about?" she says, airing her frustration at how someone could deny a child the pleasure of reading or of understanding.

At Claire's step on another day Charlie tells us that "You can't use the one and two cent coins in the shops anymore." Rosy says to him, "Is that your two cents worth for today?" and then throws in another: "That doesn't make any sense Charlie," and continues on to say, "It's nonsense if you ask me." I join in and suggest to Charlie that he "stop making sense", and we play on with the words. The meaning of money is played off against the meaning of meaning. Charlie goes off and I am left with Rosy and her sister, who is trying to get her own housing situation sorted. When she approached him on the estate, the man from the council had told her, "I don't have these conversations on the street," closing down the conversation with the words of an official in a position of authority. After we discuss this, they share a smoke back and forth and talk about when they were younger and, in particular, their deep attachment to their mother and the rituals that took place around food in the flat. They describe to me an eidetic scene from their flat on a Sunday morning:

> 'We would prepare the Sunday dinner while our ma went for a glass of Guinness to the pub. The peas had to be steeped in the pot with the white tablet from the night before. Real peas, not the shite that you get now. Before leaving the pub she would say now you go ahead and heat everything up and then when she had the dinner she would have a lie down for a couple of hours and when she got up she had to have a large pot of tea waiting for her.' (Rosy)

This story has a connection to the products that people used as they tell me. "The milk has to be Premier. The butter has to be Dairygold and the peas have to be Marrowfat." On the subject of food they tell me that other people in the block would be fed with the remainder of a meal. The feeding of those who can't or don't have the wherewithal to feed themselves is a common but delicate practice. Stories of food are common, and soon after I hear Steph and Janet talk about cooking liver and kidney and whether they go into a stew or a coddle. When he hears this, Charlie asks, in a reference to Joyce, "Isn't it liver that is in the breakfast in Ulysses?"

Sometimes these reminiscences reach deep into family events and histories and have a sharper edge. Rosy and Steph exchange stories of their family histories on outings to the religious house one day. Rosy says that her grandmother was widowed in her twenties, leaving her with Rosy's mother as her only child. She remarried and had two more children, both of whom subsequently moved to England in search of work. One of these had a child himself from a relationship and subsequently asked his mother to rear the child in Ireland. This child became the last remaining child in the house of Rosy's grandparents' family home and in the end inherited the house. Rosy says that this was because her grandmother died before her husband. Rosy believes that, had it been the other way round, Rosy's mother would have inherited the house and this would have spread the gift to many more branches on the family tree. Steph has a similar story of lost inheritance that she tells me as we walk back from the religious house. Steph had a child when she was young who was raised in her parents' home. She tells me that her family were housed in a council house that was located in a quite affluent part of the city. They bought the house from the council over time, and the value, like in many other places, subsequently increased enormously over a period of years. Steph says that she helped out, giving significant amounts of money to upgrade the house, usually working through her father, as her relationship with her mother, as she describes it, was tortuous. Steph's father died before her mother, and not long after this the house was sold for a lot of money. Steph says that almost all of the money from the sale of the house went to Steph's estranged son, who was Steph's mother's choice for succession. Such recall and memories are not confined to one's waking life. Like Charlie's bats, they infiltrate the nocturnal psyche as well, as Rosy tells me one day that when she drinks too much she has dreams of the dead and they come to her in her sleep. "I am dreaming of all my family [members] who are dead, they are coming to me when I am asleep. Almost every night when I go asleep I am dreaming about them."

Stories that reach down into family histories are complemented by those of proverbial form using words and phrases that carry lessons about petty greed and covetousness. Rosy uses stories and aphorisms as a way to understand, and often condemn, what she sees as meanness and 'grabbin'' or a lack of generosity. They carry a moral message of sorts. The subject of meanness and sharing is deep in people's lives and comes up repeatedly and can manifest itself around any number of things such as cigarettes, clothes, money, to name but some. At Tina's step one day the subject arises again, and Rosy is engaged about people who take things they don't need and who take advantage of the generosity of others. It is during this verbal passage that she rolls out the following phrases:

'When God was giving out noses, you thought he said roses and you said I'll have a big red one.'

'When God was giving out teeth, you thought he said sweets and you said I'll have a few black ones.'

'If you told her you were going to the moon, she'd say will you get me something there.' (Rosy)

The lines pick away at people who want too much, which is perhaps driven by desperation. Rosy implies that they want things so much that they end up undoing and damaging themselves as a result of their own desire and manipulation. Proverbs and sayings have become conscious and talked about probably because I have been asking people what they mean, and this continues in the community café one day. We are sitting round and people have just finished their food and are drinking tea. One of the workers uses the phrase "Have you no bell on your bike?" which provokes Rosy to comes up with the phrase "The man who made time made plenty," and she then says, "Where is last year's snow?" as a follow-up. They are lines that incite thought about the nature and passing of time. Someone uses the phrase "As the crow flies", and for once Rosy says she doesn't get it. "What do you mean how the crow flies?" she asks. On another day when we are going to the religious Steph rings Rosy to tell her that she can't make it and asks her to see if they will give Rosy a food bag for Steph. Rosy looks at me and says "What the fuck, John? Am I a fucking marshmallow? You don't do that. The only time that I ever done that was when me friend passed away and then someone got it for me. I couldn't ask someone to do that. I told you I am a fucking marshmallow." I take it that she means she is soft and easy to manipulate, but the phrase says it more clearly than any interpretation.

On a warm, late, summer's afternoon there is a gathering of sorts around Meg's step. I can see it developing as I chat with Finn across the block. I make my way over and there are a number of deckchairs arranged in a circle between the step and the footpath. There are a number of people there and some sitting on the step while others are on the chairs. I grab an empty deckchair and Meg asks me, "Would you take me grave as quick?" but she doesn't push and leaves me alone in the chair and I pick up the slow train of conversation. Meg, Rosy and Debbie talk about women using Botox and how some of the women in the estate post photos of themselves on Facebook pouting newly inflated lips. Debbie, who is on her way home from work, asks, "What the fuck would you want to look like that for?" She talks of meeting another woman who had, as she says, "come into a few bob" and asked her, "Did you have work done?" The woman told her that she had had her lips and her forehead done recently. She contorts and stretches her own face in a way that makes people laugh. She says that she would like to have her "laughing lines" done and then says, "I've cried enough in me life too." Debbie changes the subject and slags Rosy about the man in her life who shows up occasionally. "What's the story with dial a ride? Have you seen him lately?" she asks Rosy. Rosy comes back with, "And what about rent a dick? Have you seen him lately?" It's a draw, and they laugh at the unpredictable episodic nature of their love lives and the rarity of romantic love. Of the man in question, Rosy says of him on more than one occasion, "He always says to me, 'It is what it is'. What the fuck does that mean, it is what it is? Tell me will ya, for fuck's sake."

Debbie moves on to a story about a day when Rosy went with her to a play venue for children where Debbie's sister was hosting a birthday party for her child. When Rosy met Debbie's sister, she had introduced herself to Debbie's sister with the phrase "Is your mammy in? Is your daddy working?" Rosy had used this phrase in conversation with Debbie's sister while the kids were playing. Debbie's sister didn't really get it and asked Debbie in a sidebar, "What the fuck is that all about? Is your mammy in is your daddy working? Does she not know our Da is dead?" Debbie had to explain to her sister that this was just Rosy's banter. Even though I had heard her use the phrase many times before, I ask Rosy what it means, and she explains that the origins of the phrase are in the past. She says that this particular phrase was used by "people from the social welfare" when they made unannounced house visits in years past, seeking to discover if men in the estate were in fact working when they were claiming benefit. According to Rosy, the phrase "Is your mammy in, is your daddy working?" was often put to unsuspecting children as soon as a child opened the door. Officials, like child catchers of old, often did this in the hope that a child would innocently respond with information about if and where their fathers were working. The phrase has been kept alive by Rosy and is used now more for laughs, with only a residue of the original stress remaining. Debbie's sister took Rosy's question literally. She didn't know the rules of having a laugh, as it were, or how the state worked in the past, nor had she ever been asked the question.

At a bingo session in the local community centre one Saturday night the numbers are being called and the event is in full flow. People are engrossed in marking their books. I had been given a quick introduction before the start as to how to mark the bingo book, given I had never played serious bingo like this before. I have two books and Charlie is marking three books to my right. One of these is for Janet. Rosy is to my left and Janet is across the table, sitting beside Rosy's niece who tells us about going to the 'Big Time Bingo' in big venues where it costs €40 to play for a night. Charlie says that he has seen some people mark five bingo books simultaneously.

I am struggling to mark two as the game takes off. Bottles of beer are being sold four for a tenner, which Rosy says is good value compared to what they charge you in the pub. It is still too dear, as she has her own beer in her bag that she has brought with her, as has almost everyone around the table. A woman from the neighbourhood acts as MC and charges headlong through the games. "Lines and houses, lines and houses," she shouts, outlining the objective of the game. The room is almost all women, with a few men present. I wonder if bingo is a safe place for women away from men. The event is a fundraiser for the local dance group. In the institution that is bingo many of the numbers have linguistic counterparts. They are part of the culture of the game and everyone seems to know the whole set. Forty-five is "half way there." Twenty-one is the "key of the door." "Top of the House" is number ninety. "Jack's big boots" is number twelve. These number–word associations are made continuously over the course of the night. Image and number are replayed again and again, and as games end winners are announced who come to take prizes from the stage and new games begin. When the number fifty is called the entire hall breaks spontaneously and without cue into a brief rendition of the theme from the original *Hawaii Five-O* television series and sings in unison: 'De de de deh deh, de de de deh. De de de deh deh. De de de deh.' The sound rises and grows to a crescendo in the hall and then stops instantly at a movement of the MCs hand that the next number is up. There is a huge buzz in the room at this as a sense of collective expression and participation takes over the room briefly. As the night is reaching its climax, the caller calls out number ten and gives its linguistic counterpart as "a cock and hen". The hall is silent for a moment until a woman at an adjacent table shouts out, "I'll have the cock but not the hen." The room takes a second to take in the line, and then everyone erupts into laughter that takes a little while to die down. Someone says, "Ah sure, it's only Bridie for fuck sake, what d'ya expect?"

Rosy isn't having much luck with the bingo. She is talking a lot and Janet is not too impressed and there is a needle between them. Rosy uses a number of phrases consecutively at this point relating to her lack of fortune. She rolls them out with brief pauses between them as she looks dejectedly around the room. "I wouldn't get a kick in a stampede." Pause, and then, "I wouldn't get a ride in a brothel." Pause again and, "If he owned Switzerland he wouldn't give me a slide." Pause, "If he had a garden full of mickeys he wouldn't give me a look over the wall." There are others that come a little later, including, "The tide wouldn't take me out," and "I wouldn't get a date from a calendar." The lines and metaphors carry a variety of connotations from the sexual to the self-deprecating, but it is the range and repertoire of images of slides and stampedes and brothels that sticks in the mind after the words have dissipated. Oddly enough, I win on the last game. The last prizes left are 'combination sets' of washing powder, softener and bathroom cleaning products wrapped in decorative plastic, with a big red bow. All of the items are super jumbo. Janet also wins on the last game. I give Rosy my prize and she is effusive in her thanks. The prizes are utilitarian and somewhat gendered, but are nonetheless highly valued. Rosy immediately thinks who she will share the powder with. The last game of the night in a room full of women is called 'last man standing', where the 90 numbers are all called in random fashion and each person in the room has one of these numbers. The person who has the ninetieth number called wins. Rosy, Charlie and myself are in with a shout until the last three, and the prize in a room full of women is won by the only other man present.

While arguing with Charlie one day at the local shops because he was complaining about how much time things were taking, Rosy turns to Charlie and says, "You're some ball of wool. Who rolled you up?" The phrase condenses much into a few words, not least of which is the challenge of how to unpack and unravel the complexity of a (male) personality and what that entails, as well as the process of personality and psychic formation that goes into constituting an individual. Charlie doesn't even bother to try to come back on it. He has had his own struggles with literacy and reading. Speaking of his early school experiences on Tina's step one day he says to me and Rosy,

> 'I could read and write but I couldn't speak so they sent me to the school in —. I didn't read until I was 13 or 14. I learned myself to read. I was listening to my brother reading and I was looking at words on the page and that's how I learned to read. Every day I had to go the — hospital to see a speech therapist and I used to get a clip round the ear when I didn't say the world properly.' (Charlie)

He has been trying to fill this deficit by challenging himself to read a range of materials and sources, and has made progress. This practice of reading and the ambivalent feelings and memories it arouses in Charlie feeds through a conversation in the community café one afternoon when Charlie and I sit at a table with Harry, a long-time opiate user and recent convert to crack, at one of the lunch tables before the others arrive. Charlie tells Harry about the book he is reading called *Wildchild* (Croghan, 2014), about the life of a young man growing up in 1980s Dublin. The book chronicles the man's chaotic life as a teenager and his conflictual relationship with the criminal justice system. Charlie describes the major incidents in the book, including one where the author writes that his mother was assaulted when she turned up at a police station to see what was happening to him. He explains to Harry how the writer used different names instead of people's real names. Harry becomes very animated when he hears this and says with force that he himself is an avid reader. "I'm always readin," he says. I have often seen Harry sitting amid people waiting at the local bus shelter reading, or with some pulp fiction under his arm outside the local shops when he is "tappin" for money, as he calls it. Harry says that he has been writing his own life story about his life on the streets and tells Charlie that when you change people's names you give them pseudonyms. He breaks the word into syllables, "soo-doh-nims", and says them in slow motion for our benefit. "You do that because you can't write people's real names," he says. (He is also unconsciously underlining a research problematic.) Harry asks Charlie, "Do you know what the word 'brick' means in prison slang?" Before he has a chance to answer, he tells him that the more 'brick' a 'screw' has, the higher up the ladder he is. "Three brick is high up," he says. When we are outside on the street afterwards other users of the café comment on Harry's prodigious reading. Someone says, "Unbelievable what he reads." Harry's reading while homeless has a sort of mythic status in that someone living on the street could possibly sustain a reading habit alongside a drug habit in this fashion. But he has and he does. His reading has become a matter of public record and comment. Charlie's engagement in the conversation is an assertion that he too is part of the literate working class.

The local barber lends Steph a book of stories one day. It is called *Stories That Were Overheard on the Luas*, the light rail system that traverses the city. The word Luas also means light in the Irish language. Steph reads one of them out as we sit on the step outside Tina's flat:

'A woman is in court and the judge asks her to repeat what the man said to her. "Oh, I couldn't," she says. He asks her to write it down and hands her some paper and she is still pausing. "Is there a problem?" he asks. "Is there one or two Ls in bollox?" she asks.' (Steph)

Soon after, we leave the block smiling, humoured by the joke.

PART II

Critical realism and public housing

10

From manifest phenomena to generative structures

Given the ethnographic thrust of this book, one could be forgiven for thinking that events and experiences are solely what constitute reality on the Bridgetown Estate. The lay narratives and practices of residents are undoubtedly critical in that they provide a window into a world, as it were. But I want to build on and to explore the meaning of these 'thick descriptions' (Geertz, 2017) of everyday phenomena and practices, and also to add to and even challenge the ethnographic perspective as possessing the whole or sole truth, as it were. It is perhaps worth reiterating Sayer's (2000, p 149) point from Chapter 1, when he says, 'Grasping the whole is more difficult than grasping what happens next in the story.' In the move from such manifest phenomena to generative structures things are perhaps not as obvious as they appear. Culture and structure, or, to put it another way, the episodic and the configurational (Sayer, 2000, pp 142–143) are dialectically related in that practices of Bridgetown residents have roots, and perhaps make sense only in the context of their grounding and placement within social structure (Yeung, 1997; De Cocteau, 2012). This relationship between social action and (the reproduction or transformation of) social structure is outlined by Bhaskar (2009, p 133), working from a transcendental critical-realist perspective, in the following way:

> social structure is neither foreign nor something chosen by agents; rather it is what they reproduce or transform in the course of the more or less routine conduct of their everyday lives, as historically specific and axiologically necessary means and media. On the T.M.S.A. (Transformative Model of Social Action) social life, in virtue of its recursive quality, possesses a fundamentally non-teleological dynamic, in as much as agents reproduce or transform, for the most part (but not necessarily) in an unconscious and unmotivated way, the very structures they must draw upon and utilise, and which they are constrained and frustrated by, in their substantive practical productive activities. And it enables us to accept both the 'objective' and 'subjective' aspects of social existence without illicitly conflating them.

Because such social structures are 'necessarily unperceivable' and only 'show themselves in their effects' I want to try to test and to use the theoretical idea that is at the heart of transcendental critical realism, that while social reality is (partly) constituted by what we (can) observe or what we (can) experience/what happens in events, as it were, there is significantly more to social reality than experience and events. In realist theory that which can be observed and experienced is defined as the domain of the *empirical*, and that which constitutes happenings or events is defined as the domain of the *actual*. By contrast, the *real* is defined as the realm of generative mechanisms, tendencies and powers that operate at a deeper level of a stratified reality that encompasses all three levels of empirical, actual and real. It is a mind-independent intransitive reality that exists independently of us and our knowledge of which can be fallible (Bhaskar, 2008a, 2009, 2015). Sayer (2000, p 12) puts it in the following way: 'The real refers to the structures and powers of objects, the actual refers to what happens if and when those powers are activated, the empirical is defined as the domain of experience' (Bhaskar, 2008a, pp 21–62). Looked at in this way from a realist perspective, a public housing estate like the Bridgetown Estate is a prism that is constituted by and through a vector of forces many of which are never visible or perceptible, but that nonetheless have profound effects. It is usually only when (and if) we have had time to trace back and to piece things together causally that we might begin to understand in a coherent way the nature and effects of changes such as those in the changing nature of paid work or gender roles, for example. Such processes are inherently contingent, in that what happens could have happened differently and could do so in the future. From a realist perspective, then, the world is open and contingent and is not predetermined in a series of law-like, successionist regularities that say that what happened once will more than likely happen again. Social reality, rather, is 'emergent', and non-predictable, in that the way things or conditions are now could be different (Collier, 1994, pp 107–137). Social objects can and do have emergent properties. The world is therefore 'stratified' and has 'ontological depth' reaching down below surface appearances (empirical) and the activation of powers (actual), and understanding 'its essence' (in non-essentialist, contingent fashion), according to Bhaskar (2015, p 13), 'lies in the movement at any one level from knowledge of manifest phenomena to knowledge of the structures that generate them'.

Sayer (2000, p 12) uses the example of labour power to make clear these distinctions. Labour power is a capacity, a tendency that exists whether it is exercised or not (the real), and is a causal power inherent within the human species. A *potentia* or potentiality, so to speak. When it is used it becomes something transformative that is actualised (the actual), that in turn becomes something we experience or is an experience in itself (the empirical). Such potential or causal powers as that which exists in the real of labour power can be exploited for surplus value or profit, as it often is when actualised; but it can also be a causal power for transformation or emancipation or for the good, because of empirical experience that leads to the growth of class-consciousness and demands for better wages and conditions, or even for change of, or abolition of, the capitalist system itself. Those who labour could potentially make what they needed instead of making what the market demands.

By understanding that the world is contingent and stratified and has this ontological depth, it helps to make greater sense of what we see and experience and to understand that what we see and/or experience may be produced and/or affected by mechanisms that may be unobservable but are not necessarily unknowable. The Bridgetown Estate is what is manifest, but what is manifest is produced, as it were, by generative structures of class and gender mechanisms that are manifest only in their effects. As Bhaskar (2009, p 92) notes, to get at and understand the workings of such mechanisms, a transcendental-realist approach works 'in a continually iterative process of the identification, description, explanation and redescription of deeper strata of reality'. This methodology involves tracing phenomena back from what is observed to identifying and describing (and, where possible, changing by way of 'explanatory critique' and social action) causal mechanisms and structures. Taking this cue, I am trying to understand the significance of the processes and structures that are connected causally to the manifest phenomena that I have been writing about in the preceding chapters. Viewed from a realist perspective, then, public housing estates are examples of spaces where the real, the actual and the empirical exist and flow simultaneously. Penetrating, shaping and underpinning the empirical and the actual day-to-day lives of residents is the real of class relations, the real of gender relations and all of that which takes place in chorological space and chronological time. The nature of life on the Bridgetown Estate is, has been and will be affected by different influences and mechanisms such as the actions of systemic changes in capitalism, the role of the state or everyday tenant struggles. In this way, public housing estates are open systems that are affected and influenced not just by one mechanism or process (Sayer, 2000, p 15; Resnick and Wolff, 1987) but by many, some of which may be empirically observable (as happens in economic crisis with particular policy changes in education or welfare, for instance), and some which are not. Some mechanisms may also be in contradiction or pulling against each other, as when the policies of austerity or the demands of capitalism collide with social rights or the needs for love and care in the affective domain. The real of life on the Bridgetown Estate, as I understand it and will argue, is made and reproduced in the interlocking and intersectionality of material, affective and spatial mechanisms that combine and operate to produce the particular class forms and manifestations of the preceding chapters. The struggles that people engage in for the 'goods' of valued ways of life, for food, work, money, for love and care over time and in space are structured by such mechanisms, and also tend toward reproducing particular class and gender forms even when such outcomes are not predetermined.

Three themes

In order to pick up this thread of necessary relations, I will focus on three major themes that have emerged from this work. The first is that for people who live on the Bridgetown Estate life is a *practical–material struggle* determined largely by their particular position within class and gender structures. They are 'thrown' into this world and land in *pre-existing* sets of necessary relations within a capitalist–patriarchal society that tends toward reproducing such structures even if the future is open. The position, place or location that a person or group occupies in *class relations* and *class processes* therefore has critical significance as to what happens and is likely to happen, despite the best efforts of individuals. The second theme is that people are *affective embodied beings* who carry with them the emotional and psychological effects of class and gender encapsulated within the singular organism that makes up body and mind. The affective world of the Bridgetown Estate is largely driven and sustained by women. There are deep struggles over love and care to try to ensure that children and family and friends are cared for and emotionally sustained. For life itself and for commodity production to be possible, the social and emotional reproduction (Dalla Costa, 1995; Ahmed, 2008; Federici, 2010; Ferguson, 2020; Lynch, 2022) of the species must take place, and, with it, all of the nurturing and care that this entails. Despite the burden and stress of the manifest struggles that residents engage in, relations and emotions of love and care underpin the social structure of the Bridgetown Estate. Written deep into bodies and minds (Adair, 2002) are the markings and inscriptions of class in that bodies are broken down prematurely by things such as work, both paid or unpaid, institutional neglect or abuse, sexual assault, violence and addiction (Marsh, 2020). As Archer (2000, p 7) describes it, this is 'the nexus of our embodied relations with the world'. Therefore, while class still remains fundamentally a product of the economic and social relations people engage in, it also has deep affective roots and consequences that affect and shape the emotional–psychic lives of estate residents. The corporeal has sensuous psychic extension in that there are also lifelong struggles over learning and expression, part of which is that words can occasionally have a somewhat redemptive power. Third, and critically for this work, these struggles are *lived out in place and through time.* In other words, class happens somewhere in that it has spatiality, temporality and history. Class is *in* the world. Yes, class is under the skin and in the psyche (Kuhn, 1995; Cruz, 2021), but it is also in the streets and communities of the city and nation-state and the world. Public housing estates are particular social forms, for particular groups of people, just like the workhouse or the poorhouse were in the past, or the Traveller halting site is in the present. Being, time and space are knitted together in a continuum as such. They will become the historical objects and curiosities of the future. The Bridgetown Estate is a physical signifier and referent-object that shows us how the nature and production of space (Lefebvre, 1991) is deeply classed. The city is a class text of buildings, streets and empty spaces to be read and deciphered, if we are to understand its real nature.

All three of these themes express the idea that for residents of the Bridgetown Estate how they live is both an outcome and a presupposition of the sets of relations they engage in and the nature of those relations, whether they be defined by struggles over exploitation, domination and injustice or by relations of love, care and solidarity or by residents' relation to the city. The challenge is therefore in making visible or obvious the nature of such relations and how they are constituted and maintained in building a bridge between the empirical the actual and the real of life on the Bridgetown Estate. (Theoretical) explanations as to why things are the way they are therefore very important. For example, there are various voluntarist–individualist explanations that place the emphasis or responsibility on the individual for her or his own failure or success. Life conditions are deemed to be the product, result or outcome of individual choice or preference, and therefore there is no reason or cause to protest or to complain, because a life is deemed to be wholly the result of the actions, or lack of, of the individual. To be free in liberal thought is to be free to enter into contracts with other individuals. This is a prominent view in much of liberal-individualist economics, sociology and philosophy, and is also the ideology and basis of the 'calculative sobriety' (Coles and Haro, 2019) of the neoliberal worldview (Harvey, 2005; Brown, 2015). And while there are many variations on this theme it is perhaps best encapsulated in the idea of humans as Rational Economic Actors (Folbre and Hartmann, 1989) driven by singular instrumental means–end rationalities. This sort of logic presupposes that there will always be winners and losers in what is presented as a fair, meritocratic contest. If one is a loser in the contest the cause(s) can be found only within oneself. Within such a worldview the generators of social conditions, the essential relations that are a product of key sets of social and economic relationships are therefore denied any purchase or relevance in the situation that in effect acts to conceal the very nature of those relations. But such generative causes and mechanisms are critically important, for they are often unobservable or simply not visible. But, as is clear from previous chapters, the clues are all over this work.

11

Class as the production of scarcity: wage, price, debt, food

Scarcity is a profound and common characteristic of working-class life. It assumes the characteristics of doxa (Bourdieu, 1977, pp 159–71) or common sense (Gramsci, 2005, pp 323–377) and, while people feel it and often refer to it, difficulties remain in getting people to talk about it. Even its existence is contentious (see Ferriter, 2005, p 7). As Steph or Rosy or others say, "That's just the way it is." Or as Michelle says, "Whatever hand you are dealt, you just have to get on with it." My contention here is that the scarcity that is evident in this study is a product of the class positions and necessary relations that people find themselves in as an outcome of living in a capitalist society. In other words, it is neither accidental nor is it innate to individuals. A society that tethers its material and immaterial production to the private accumulation of wealth inexorably produces such graphic inequalities (Dorling, 2015; Streeck, 2017; Savage, 2021). This inevitably produces winners and losers, and in such monetised wealth stakes the people of the Bridgetown Estate are the losers. This produces particular forms of class-consciousness or what Raymond Williams described as 'structures of feeling'. And while the liminal boundaries between classes may be fuzzy (Bourdieu and Wacquant, 1992), social classes share what Bourdieu called homologous or common conditions of existence that are outcomes of world historical class processes (Wallerstein, 1983). The Bridgetown Estate is inhabited by an objective social class sharing generally common conditions of existence (Weber, 1978, pp 926–940; Savage et al, 1992; Olin Wright, 1997; pp 34–37, 2015; Bourdieu, 2000, p 101; Umney, 2018). This is perhaps clearest from the nature of the work both paid and unpaid that people do, their subordinate and antagonistic position within class relations and their general state of propertylessness as a group. The nature of such conditions is evident at the empirical level in that the daily struggle for material survival is the font and origin of almost all practices on the estate. Consciousness is defined by practical struggles and efforts to overcome or to come to terms with scarcity and lack. In this sense it dominates and permeates life on the Bridgetown Estate. It determines the nature of being and practices and is a principle or axis around which life rotates as it flows through time.

Scarcity manifests itself in many ways, one of which is in struggles to find paid work that pays a 'decent wage' that might lessen hardship and possibly be interesting or stimulate a person. The wage and struggles for a better wage and working conditions are and have been central to Frank's existence. He is but one of many possible examples, and his life is one of continuous struggle against scarcity that has been defined and shaped by the peaks and troughs of work in various industries in modern capitalist Ireland. He has been umbilically connected to this world of paid work since he started working at 15. He is subject to what Hochschild (2000, p 46) calls 'the new rhythms of work'. This relation has been one of base necessity, and also became one of personal identity and class pride. It has also been very much characterised by antagonism between worker and employer. He is very much the conflicted male 'working class hero' that Caplan (2004) writes about, a possible character from *Brassed Off*, *The Full Monty*, *Billy Elliot*, someone who has engaged passionately in strikes and class struggles against capital in various places and sites, and yet the demands of capital have overwhelmed him in the end, in that the older he gets he can no longer keep up with what is required of him by the company (see Gibson Graham, 2006, pp 1–21). Younger men were brought in to replace him and he became completely alienated from his own labour, due to the nature of the worker–employer nexus and the incessant demands for more productivity and the creation of more surplus value. Like almost everyone else on the estate, his life is defined by a state of propertylessness, in that he owns nothing except his labour power and some basic possessions. His self-identity is thoroughly interwoven with his sense of himself as a hard worker. There were occasional periods when work was abundant, but his life maps closely, and was deeply affected by the prolonged austerity visited upon Ireland and internationally in recent years, when he was unemployed for almost seven years continuously after the economic crash. If the structure was global capitalism, the mechanism of disciplining and punishing the working class was austerity (Hall and Massey, 2011; Allen, 2012, 2013; Bissett, 2015; Coulter and Nagle, 2015; O Callaghan et al, 2015; O Riann, 2015; Statement of UN Special Rapporteur, 2018). Frank became, and not for the first time, part of what Braverman once described as the industrial reserve army of labour. And if we trace further back beyond this recent past there is also the longer historical arc of the lives of residents such as Frank and Nadia that track these changes through the disappearance over decades of the industrial and manufacturing base that once existed in the spaces of the adjacent hinterland of the city. The closure and exporting of such industries to countries with cheaper labour sources saw the arrival of newer and in many ways more insecure and, in Frank's case, more brutal forms of employment. The precariat may be a recently developed concept (Standing, 2011) fusing together prec-arious with prolet-ariat, but precarity is and was an ever-present experientiality for estate residents. As Frank discovered when paid work began to reappear after the economic crisis, the relationship and the quid pro quo between capital and labour had changed once again, the shift significantly favouring those with capital. He is well aware of the 'unwarranted advantages that were accruing to certain protagonists' and that 'the wage profit ratio again began to benefit capital.' (Boltanski and Chiapello, 2005, pp 176, 178). The rate of exploitation has intensified for those at the bottom, as has the extraction of effort and surplus value. Frank is fully aware of the exploitative core of worker–capitalist class relations and his own casual disposability. He knows that there is a continuous attempt to make labour cheaper to employers and that he is living in an era of 'cheap work' (Patel and Moore, 2020, pp 91–110). He has come to see himself as just another inanimate resource from which to extract value. He has lived it and understood it and he talks to it and about it relentlessly, every day. He knows that the work *contract* is a fiction, because he has lived it. The nature or 'spirit' of capitalism and its contingent manifestations has undergone fundamental changes and discontinuities during the lives of Frank and Nadia . The knowledge Frank possesses of how things were in the past in comparison with the present contrasts with the current lack of knowledge that young people have of this past in the present. His is a politicised class-consciousness that has been made through struggle. Dialectically interposed with the relationality of class, therefore, is its *contingent historicity and form* over time (Streeck, 2017, pp 201–225). Frank's life reflects the dynamic nature of class relations as they change and are reformulated through struggles between capital and labour over time. Class is much more of a dynamic relational process between groups than it is merely a position or location in the system of production or a gradational income or census scale (Bourdieu, 1987; Savage, 2013). It is the glue that binds the latticework of capitalist social relations through space–time. His life and that of the estate is implicitly one replete with a (changing) class history, most of which has never been framed as such or described as such (Coulter, 1999; Ferriter, 2005; Silverman, 2006; Allen, 2013). And yet, despite the shift to a neoliberal capitalism and a post-industrial world, and the profundity of the change, such capital–labour relations still remain pivotal to estate life even if they have taken on new forms. This remains the case even if the level of class-consciousness or the sense of a class for itself with some form of collective political identity has dissipated in the present, as is reflected in Frank's frustration with younger workers like Conor.

Scarcity and lack produce particular effects on one's existence and consciousness, one of which operates in the realm of consumption and is an obsession and anxiety with price, and therefore with money. Whether it is a medical prescription, toilet rolls, a haircut (the list is almost endless), price matters crucially. One of the most-used phrases among people is 'How much is that?' It is need and minimal resources, and not instrumental economic rationality that underpins such obsessions. Writing about the significance of class in her life as a poor Black American woman who joined the upper middle-class through her academic prowess but was still largely unaccepted, bell hooks (2000, p 61) explores how such monetary anxieties and obsessions differed between people from her own working-class origins and the privileged middle class:

> most of the poor and working class folks in our neighbourhood talked freely about money. Everyone talked about how much things cost. When I entered worlds where individuals were materially privileged, now and then I would ask about the cost of material objects they had purchased, and again I would be told by someone, who would take me aside, that it was not polite to talk about how much things cost.

Attention to price here does not denote a lack of consciousness of universal value, as is often presumed, that is, as one of Oscar Wilde's characters says, knowing the price of everything and the value of nothing. In fact, it perhaps attributes even more value to things than they deserve. Such effects burrow deep into the psyche and the everyday struggles as to whether one has the money to pay bills or rent and, on occasion, to pay for necessities such as milk and bread or for cigarettes or a child's birthday party. In general, one *must* find the cheapest option. Responses to such financial struggles have brought about the development of informal practices and systems of borrowing and lending between people and within groups. These informal *reciprocal credit* economies sustain people from day to day and from week to week. There are no written records or ledgers in this informal system, people simply carry mental promissory notes as to what is owed and when it will be paid back. If there were a way to calculate the amounts of money that flow through this informal system, I think it would reveal substantial volumes. These are also non-exploitative, interest-free credit systems in which it would be unthinkable to charge interest rates to friends or neighbours. These practices operate outside of the formal credit system, and those who lend one week can be borrowing the next. These social credit systems highlight a consciousness of the precariousness of the existence of others and oneself and a willingness to help each other out in this way. Instead of the exchange of gifts or a kula ring (Mauss, 1990), it is money that is borrowed, to be paid back later. Such alternative economic practices also indicate the importance that people place on trying to keep themselves and others free from institutional and perhaps all types of debt (Graeber, 2011). That this is not always possible is evident in the persona of the money lender, working for a large lending company, offering 'ninja' loans when the needs are greater than can be met within the social circle of the group. He has significant capital to lend, and he is desperately looking for borrowers who will give him a return on this capital. This proves Marx's point that capitalists come in many shapes and forms, from employers to lenders to rentiers to retailers to investors/speculators. The rates of interest on such loans depict the intense level of exploitation that is attached to them. Practices of informal lending and borrowing between residents make it clear that people do not make contracts with each other as to what their obligations and expectations are contractually as liberal individualism would have it. Instead, such practices are driven by relational interdependencies and forms of solidarity (Gibson Graham, 2006, p 61; Mellor, 2010; Lynch and Kalaitzake, 2020) and by sharing based on the exigencies and necessities of existence. These practices are forms of solidarity or commons lending, or 'cooring' finance, to adapt a term of inter-farm solidarity from the world of rural Ireland (Brody, 1973, pp 131–157).

On another level, scarcity generates primitive struggles to find and procure extra food resources, and, as we have seen, this involves extensive time and effort and is a form of work in itself. There is a pool of knowledge as to where food resources are available in and around the city and how to access them. The practice and necessity of securing food and the growth of food bank economies says something profound about the societies we live in (Garthwaite, 2016). COVID-19 and the war in Ukraine have intensified the need for food and have rapidly extensified these charity food systems. If there is shame attached to this process it is usually displaced using humour or suppressed so deeply within the self that it hardly seems to exist. And yet the visit to the religious house is an in-group event rarely if ever discussed in public. These food-searching practices generate debates about entitlements and forms of sharing and solidarity that are hugely important to people. They also bring about discussions as to what 'meanness' means and the effects it has on a group. For someone like Rosy not to share is anathema to being human. Not sharing is a serious threat to group cohesion and survival and this, I think, is the reason why it is condemned so strongly in various ways. Such practices may sometimes be, or appear to be, habitual or routinised, but they go deep into the emotional being of people and involve commitments and investments, and some degree of consciousness often driven by the base needs of personal and family survival. The trips to the religious house engender once again a set of necessary relationships. Instead of workers and employers, there are possessors and non-possessors or resource commanders and resource receivers in this set. In this case there are those who possess the resource, that is, those who gatekeep and control it, and there are those such as the Bridgetown residents and others who are in a dependent position come to seek it out of need. Such practices may become habitual, but they are more than a set of predispositions. Perhaps habit(us) is another name for suppressed shame. If this sentiment were to express itself it would say something like, 'Forgive me, for I know well what I do, too well perhaps, but for particular reasons I cannot or do not want to acknowledge it publicly.' Such practices, therefore, may appear like habit or routine.

The lives and practices of Bridgetown residents are products of necessity, which manifests itself in a particular classed consciousness that is in turn generated out of sets of necessary relations, whether they are worker–capitalist relations or tenant–landlord or in relations such as those of food receiver vis-à-vis food commander/mediator. While they may or may not resign themselves to such class positions and the practices they produce, people are acutely conscious of the nature of their lives even if they do not understand clearly why their lives take the form they do. The lives of Frank and Nadia and Michelle tell us clearly that class is hugely significant in their lives and, as many others have written, *class matters* because of how it shapes and defines the contours of a life and a community (Mahony and Zmroczek, 1997; Coulter, 1999; hooks, 2000; Munck, 2007; Atkinson, 2015; Fraser, 2018; Cruz, 2021). To make such a case is to go against the grain, so to speak, in that, as we have seen, fundamental understandings of class are largely missing from analyses of public housing estates in Ireland. In such analyses, like much of state-funded technocratic–corporatist sociology in Ireland, class exists only as a reified and static 'socio-economic category' or slot. These are what Olin Wright (1997, p 34) called 'gradational' conceptions of class, and in such conceptions class is only a list of positions on a scale. It has no real existence as a dynamic relational entity within which lives are shaped and determined by the nature and structure of relations of ownership and power between groups. When much of what is written does not acknowledge, much less understand, the existence of class in this relational sense, then class is non-existent or negated. It becomes reduced to a term such as 'socio-economic category'. And if it has no real existence, then things remain as they are, in that the status quo is eternalised and those in privileged class positions claim that they are there on merit and on hard work. Questions of inequalities of distribution or recognition simply do not exist, or do not get raised (see Fraser and Honneth, 2003; Baker et al, 2004), and hierarchy becomes, to all intents and purposes, the 'natural' order of things. The real nature of relations as to why groups occupy particular class positions remains mystified and inchoate. The preceding chapters show clearly that class matters and has critical import for the lives of the Bridgetown residents. This is as true of the present as it was of the past, and conceivably for the future if there is no substantial change. The invisibilising and ideological mystification of class cannot conceal this, nor can it be allowed to do so. The lives of Bridgetown residents prove that class and class relations matter now more than ever.

12

Women and the affective domain of the Bridgetown Estate

Understanding class in a practically adequate manner is therefore crucially important, and particularly as to how it relates to gender. In her work on the experiences of working-class mothers in England, Diane Reay (1998a, p 272) argues strongly that class matters crucially in a material sense, but she also makes the case for a more expansive understanding of what class is that extends from beyond the economic into a qualitative emotional world: 'Class is a complicated mixture of the material, the discursive, psychological predispositions and sociological predispositions that quantitative work on class location and class identity cannot hope to capture.'

Under particular conditions and within specific class-based contexts, we develop relations to ourselves and to others. The struggles over daily necessity just described in the previous chapter have a strong gendered dimension in that life takes a particular form for men like Charlie, Frank and Karl where they are usually trying to get themselves from week to week, living out relatively conventional masculine identities. But for women like Michelle, Rosy, Steph, Nadia and Tina, they are carrying the responsibility for children and grandchildren and their well-being over a lifetime, as well as trying to provide the basic necessities of life. It is clear from this study that the provision of care and relations of dependency and interdependency are central to their lives and to the life of the Bridgetown Estate. A broad range of feminist theory (Gilligan, 1982; Tronto, 1994; Sevenhuijsen, 1998; Kittay, 1999; Crean, 2018; Lynch, 2020, 2022) makes the point that dependency and interdependency are innately part of the human condition. Despite everything, including all of the material struggles they face, there is a strong case to be made that the women of the Bridgetown Estate do in fact speak a lot of the time in and with 'a different voice' (Gilligan, 1982) and operate from 'an ethic of care' (Tronto, 1994) or act with what Crean (2018) describes as a 'care consciousness'. In spite of the fact that there is violence, both subjective and systemic, that they must often confront, such struggles and commitments to love and care highlight just how important such qualities are to life on the estate. In many cases women carry this burden without men. Central to all of this are the attempts by women to somehow manage and combine the worlds of unpaid and paid work. The estate has become more feminised over time, in that women now comprise 70% of the tenants on the estate, with many of them living as single parents more often without partners. What some (wrongly in my view) describe as the 'residualisation' (Power, 1999) of public housing estates is also, and perhaps more importantly, therefore a gendered story of the feminisation of class, the impoverishment of women and the alienation of female labour (Trott, 2017). As Sayer (2005) has argued, capitalism is not by necessity a source of gender oppression. Patriarchy existed long before capitalism and could well exist in a post-capitalist world, so it is important to identify the mechanism in and of itself, or the relationship between such mechanisms, if we are to attempt solutions. The fact that there was a significant clothing and textile industry that employed thousands of women, many from the Bridgetown Estate, for a number of decades reinforces the point that capitalism is not overly worried about the gender, or race for that matter, of those it exploits as long as surplus value can be extracted. This is also the case with care itself, but care is embedded in capitalist, patriarchal structures and expectations that, by and large, women will fulfil these primary caring roles and duties (Patel and Moore, 2020, pp 111–137; Lynch, 2022).

This gendered nature of the estate, and perhaps the larger public housing system and the import of such a process, is crucially important. It is arguable that it is women who largely sustain the emotional life of the Bridgetown Estate in what Lynch has called the affective domain. Lynch et al (2009, p 3) argue that the exclusive focus on the 'structuralist trilogy of class, status and power' originating in the sociologies of Marx and Weber has led to a focus on the subject being understood primarily through the categories of the economic, the social and the political, to the neglect of the affective. This focus, usually on *man* as an economic actor, has led to a neglect of the gendered affective relations without which life would be virtually meaningless. A growth of feminist theory in recent decades has challenged these 'domain assumptions' of intellectual theoretical work that quite often present problems as universal when they are quite often particular and 'male-stream'. Lynch et al (2009, p 12) argue that matters of love and care have been treated in most liberal theory as essentially private matters (Lynch et al, 2009, p 12) and that this liberal–patriarchal perspective leads to a general devaluing and marginalising of the labour of love and care that women do most of the time in both unpaid and (usually very poorly) paid capacities. Such work is therefore deemed to have little or no relation to the public sphere and to be a private matter, unless it becomes a possible source of economic value. Instead, Lynch et al (2009, p 2) argue that this view is defective, for it ignores 'the salience of care and love as goods of public significance ... and the importance of caring as a human capability meeting a basic human need'. They argue forcefully that the affective domain is important to understand in its own right because it generates two very important forms of inequality, 'inequality in the degree to which people's needs for love and care are satisfied, and inequality in the work that goes into satisfying them' (Lynch et al, 2009, p 12). These two inequalities take shape, then, around the receiving of care and the giving or doing of care. For a number of reasons, critical of which are the effects and outcomes of the structures and 'invisible mechanisms' (Lynch et al, 2009, p 29) that organise our societies, some people and groups are likely to receive more love and care than others, while some people and groups are more likely to carry a far greater burden of doing caring work than others. Relations of care operate at a personal level between care recipients and care givers, and the nature of such relations can be contingent, but relations of care are critically conditioned by the class and gender mechanisms that configure and structure the societies we live in. As neoliberal capitalism digs deeper in its efforts to extract value and to commodify all aspects of life, 'care' is viewed as another sphere of life that can be commodified and exploited as if it were an exploitable resource and 'market' like any other (Lynch, 2022). This raises important questions as to what is and is not commodifiable in relation to care. For instance, Lynch et al (2009, p 35) argue that most of what they define as 'primary care relations' within families and with those closest to us cannot be commodified. We can pay someone to care *for* someone, but we cannot make them care *about* them (Lynch et al, 2009, pp 49–52). In other words, there are limits to commodification. Skeggs (2002, pp 56–73) makes a similar point in her research into the lives of a group of working-class women carers in the north of England. Caring for someone and caring about someone are quite different things. Caring for someone can be done in an instrumental and mechanical fashion and can be carved up into units of economic time and value, whereas caring about someone involves deep emotional investment and the quality of love. But this does not stop the attempt to commodify and to exploit care as a commodity.

Struggles over care therefore, just like those over the means of life, are part and parcel of life on the Bridgetown Estate and are clearly evident in the struggles that women have engaged in through time, in many cases without the help of men. Although they have different sources, women must live and deal with the double bind of both class and gender mechanisms in that they are often managing the burdens of both unpaid and paid work. The world of unpaid work is intense and demanding and ranges across all of the different parts of 'housework', to the work of nurturing highly dependent children with little or no respite (see Reay, 1998b). If there are such things as 'surplus affection' or 'surplus love', this is where they are produced and where they generally go unacknowledged. Women like Rosy, Nadia and Michelle carry responsibility both for the reproductive–emotional work of love and care and the nurturing of children and older people and, in some cases, care of friends when they become incapacitated. They do this while also trying to find waged work when and wherever possible. Writing about the distorted understanding of 'work' that usually defines paid work as that of most importance and credibility, Gibson Graham (2006, pp 62–63) make the following point about the obverse and often unrecognised and marginalised labour of unpaid work:

> The most prevalent form of labor is the unpaid work that is conducted in the household, the family and the neighbourhood, or the wider community. While this work is unremunerated in monetary terms, many would say it does not necessarily go uncompensated. The rewards for this labor come in the form of love, emotional support, protection, companionship and a sense of self-worth. ... To include all of this work in a conception of a diverse economy is to represent many people who see themselves (or are labelled) as 'unemployed' or 'economically inactive' as economic subjects, that is, as contributing to vast skein of economic relations that make up our societies. It is also to recognize the multiple forms of work that most of us (and especially those, often women, who work the 'double day') engage in.

The gendered division of labour in the Bridgetown Estate is weighted heavily toward women carrying the additional burden of love and care. Hochschild (1983) makes a useful distinction between *emotional labour*, which has to do with women providing services with a smile in paid work, such as that of women working as hostesses in the airline industry, and *emotional work*, which is bound up with primary love and care relations with those closest to us. Women carry most of the burden of the emotional work of the estate, and many of them, like Michelle, carry heavy burdens of emotional labour too. Emotional labour is a performance and is demanded and exploited by those who are paying, while the emotional work involves commitments and personal attachments and is done in and for itself. Michelle's life or that of Nadia or that of Rosy are good examples of the double bind of trying to survive materially by finding whatever paid work or other resources they could while also trying to raise children and to care for and keep them safe in what can be a hostile environment. Nadia's life was and continues to be defined by her struggle to raise three children in a one-bedroom flat, as the sole parent, while working in many different paid jobs over this period. Very much a factory-girl-woman-on-the-line (Glucksmann, 1982), for much of her paid working life she was also a sole parent nurturing and rearing three children simultaneously in her unpaid working life. As she described it herself, without the solidarity and support of her mother and other women in similar positions in the estate, things might have completely fallen apart. To listen to Nadia and other women, children have brought great joy and a sense of purpose to their lives, but the other side to this is the toll that such work and care labour takes on people over time. The price Nadia has paid is visible in a body that is wracked with pain and contorted physically.

While she is of a younger generation, Michelle's story is much the same in that she has raised her children for almost all of their lives as a sole parent while also trying to stay in paid employment. Just like many other women on the estate, she provides care in a paid capacity as a health worker, and she provides all of the care for her children. Hers is a full-time life of care in that she goes through a revolving door from primary to secondary care relations and back again, day in day out. Until her child started school, Rosy had her child with her all of the time. In the flat, in the block, walking the streets, sourcing food, generally without respite. She was late to parenthood after a lifetime of employment, most of it part time and casual, but she struggles with the same burden as that carried by Nadia and Michelle and many other women on the Bridgetown Estate.

The effects of such work are evident in visible traces on bodies. Often unnoticed or ignored, women carry the legacy of such work in flesh and bone. As Merleau–Ponty (2014, p 96) says, 'the body is an affective object'. This is the point made by Adair and many others (see hooks, 2000; Tyler, 2008; Federici, 2010) when she too critiques a singularly Marxist or Weberian conception of class that sticks rigidly within the confines of what are usually male-focused economic categories. Like Lynch and Reay and many other feminist theorists, Adair wants to go beyond male-centred conceptions of social class such as that of Sennett and Cobb's (1993) 'hidden injuries' of male-only work, to understand fully the lives of poor working-class women in the US who are demonised and harassed by state and federal institutions, largely through a patriarchal lens and consolidation of conservative male power. Using her own life history as a base and through her own research with other poor women in the US, Adair describes how female bodies carry on their person for a lifetime the physical scars and marks of class and gendered positions, of work paid and unpaid and of scarcity and lack. Drawing on the work of Michel Foucault, and echoing Kafka's story of the penal colony, she describes how bodies function as surfaces or texts onto which are (often physically) inscribed messages confirming and reiterating their social position, subordination and immiseration: 'The bodies of poor women and children, scarred and mutilated by state mandated material deprivation and public exhibition, work as spectacles, as patrolling images socializing and controlling bodies within the body politic' (Adair, 2002, p 461).

In previous centuries it was through the 'entertainment' of public torture and ritual executions that the population was disciplined and socialised through what Foucault (1991, p 29) described in *Discipline and Punish* as a 'micro–physics of power'. They were shown what would happen to them if they transgressed the rules and norms of the society through a variety of public spectacles of torture and mutilation. Today power no longer normally operates in such a visible, ritualistic, public manner most of the time. Instead, it operates anonymously through institutions and the bureaucratic field to use Bourdieu's concept, as well as various media that makes it more difficult to penetrate its origins and workings. This is how Rosy often describes her relationship with the matriarch of the clinic she attends each day. She knows how little power she has in this relationship, because she is reminded of it regularly. She feels that she has become something of a medical object and curiosity. Michelle knows it from the staff hierarchy in the hospital where she works, when she is given orders repeatedly as to what to do and where to go. Nadia knows it from having to remain in a one-bedroom flat with three children for 40 years and having no negotiating power with the city council or freedom and the wherewithal to move in any other sphere of the housing system. Tina struggles with understanding generally, and she has been left to fend for herself by the institutions of the state, if they didn't also abandon and neglect her as a child in the first instance. The scapegoating of poor working-class women, according to Adair, is determined by different forms of power, usually by demonising them in the media or by using the institutions of the state to regulate, discipline and control how and what they can do (Ball, 2019; Blokland, 2008, 2019; Povey, 2019). This is done generally by men in positions of power in media or political institutions asserting their domination. Such technologies of power send consistent messages to women to know their place, thus leaving them to carry the burden of paid and unpaid work or the work of care ad infinitum. Rosy's radio intervention against male violence, while brave and full of sisterhood solidarity, was tightly controlled by men controlling the channels of communication. It was an aberrant, violent man who was the problem, not men or male violence in general. The bodies of Nadia, of Steph and of Rosy are fleshy testimony to the hardships of being a working-class woman living in a public housing estate. They carry with them in bodies and minds the imprints of the effects of gendered lives. Twisted limbs, distended stomachs and the physical and psychic scars of sexual violence remind them on a daily basis. So too do struggles and intense debate over issues such as male violence, much of it drug related and innate to hegemonic (Hanlon, 2012; Connell, 2018) or toxic masculinity. These struggles highlight the fact that, while not to idealise them, women like Rosy, Steph, Tina and Nadia are impassioned beings with deep commitments and investments of love and care and strong views on virtue and justice. They don't describe it like that, but that's what they live every day. They are trying desperately to keep their children and themselves free from harm, both in the present and into the future. If the future for their children and friends cannot be changed, it will not be for lack of intense effort or belief in the possibility on their part (see Reay and Lucey 2000). They have a good sense as to how things are likely to play out, as they have watched and learned how things happen. But they refuse to accept a preordained future. They are unlikely realists in this sense. Rosy's anxiety about how her child will survive in a world that is often brutal reflects this desire to protect and to nurture. She has a fierce care-consciousness (Crean, 2018) and wants her child not just to survive but to have a good life. They are actively engaged with those they love and care. They are committed to them, and these commitments are given over lifetimes. We may substitute preferences one for another but, as Sayer (2005, pp 41–42) reminds us, 'commitments imply emotional, reasoned attachment ... commitments figure prominently in the everyday struggles of social life'. Worrying that they are failing or that their children will not have decent or good lives is a constant in their thought. These practices and the idea that people value ways of living and 'goods' has been evident throughout this work, and is at odds with theories of social action that predicate humans as instrumentally driven or totally rational–habitual creatures who are predisposed to adapt themselves to the fields of power in automated, strategic fashion. As we have seen, the 'fit' between habitat and habitus is often awkward and ill fitting, and people are involved in deep ethical struggles over how to live with dignity and perhaps be able to flourish. They do not want to habituate themselves to scarcity or lack or to violence or to the place if they think life will be better somewhere else, as we saw with Maxine when she decided to leave the estate. There are intense *internal conversations* (Archer, 2000, pp 193–221; Sayer, 2005, p 29) going on in people's minds most of the time, in that they want good lives for themselves and their children. The relationality that underpins primary care relations is a different form of relationality to that which underpins social action from a Bourdieusian perspective through one's habitus, which is supposed to attune and to enculturate one to the environs and milieu one finds oneself in.

To finish this chapter, I want to engage briefly with the work of Pierre Bourdieu in that his theory and arguments have been very influential in that the origin of group practices and ways of being in the world is understood through the concept of the 'habitus', which he defines as 'the mental structures and dispositions that are inculcated into people through processes of socialisation and of education. They are systems of durable transposable dispositions ... principles of the generation and structuring of practices' (Bourdieu, 1977, p 72). The habitus operates as the connecting rod between subjective life and objective structural reality, and Bourdieu is always keen to point out that we are neither rule-following mechanistic reflections of objective structures nor are we purely Sartreian characters of free will and utter autonomous creativity. In his view, people do not merely read the lines that have already been written for them as in role theory, nor do they write the script for the drama in which they participate. Instead, they inherit, imbibe and are taught the lessons from the culture of the group through proverbs, sayings and doings, and adopt it as they go along. Bourdieu argues that we carry a 'genetic structuralism' in our social DNA that conditions us to see and respond to the world in particular ways. Based on the sort of habitus I have inherited and been socialised into I am likely or predisposed to see the world through that habitus and to act in ways that accord with that habitus also. It is my way of being. We do this sort of work. We play these sorts of sports. We watch these sorts of programmes on television. The habitus is crucially conditioned by the 'capitals' that one possesses, which come in economic, cultural and social forms that are themselves closely related to and grounded in social class (Bourdieu, 1986). The volume of capital(s) one possesses plays a key role in whether individuals and groups find themselves in dominant or subordinate positions in the social field and social structure. Different social classes have different habitus relative to the capitals they possess, which in turn is reflected in the social, economic and cultural practices they engage in and have engaged in in the past. The greater the volumes of the respective capitals one possesses, the better the hand one has and the better position one is likely to find within the many 'fields of power' that exist in social space (Bourdieu, 1989). Such practices form the foundations and bases of class 'distinction' based on taste (Bourdieu, 2000). Bourdieu's definition of an objective social class contends that, while the lines between classes may be fuzzy and have a practical logic (see Bourdieu and Wacquant, 1992) of their own, distinct social classes live under 'homologous conditions' and have 'homologous dispositions'. (Bourdieu, 2000, p 101). Bourdieu acknowledges that the habitus of a group is also deeply gendered, and in his research work on the Kabyle people in Algeria at the end of the 1960s the distinctions between male and female are embedded in the organisation, distribution and understanding of living space as well as in the psyche of villagers. The habitus of different groups and classes is a product of the fields of power that exist outside of people but are nonetheless reproduced by them from one generation to the next:

> practical evaluation of the likelihood of success of a given action in a given situation brings into play a whole body of wisdom, sayings, commonplaces, ethical precepts, ('that's not for the likes of us') and, at a deeper level, the unconscious principles of the ethos which, being the product of a learning process dominated by a determinate type of objective regularities, determines 'reasonable' and 'unreasonable' conduct for every agent subjected to those regularities. (Bourdieu, 1977, p 77)

In one of his endnotes in his *Outline of a Theory of Practice*, Bourdieu elaborates more on this saying that the habitus 'designates a way of being, a habitual state, (especially of the body) and in particular a predisposition, tendency, propensity or inclination' (Bourdieu, 1977, p 214). Bourdieu's work has been critiqued (see Ranciere, 1991; Jenkins 2002; Sayer, 2005) for its particular focus on social action as a strategic game of anticipation (protention is his term for this, taken from Merleau Ponty) in which individuals and groups struggle to retain advantage or privilege or even to remain where they are in the social hierarchy vis-à-vis other groups. They develop a 'feel for the game' and where and how they should fit within it. They are also 'caught' within the game, in that they do not fully understand that they are operating within fields of power in that the rules pre-exist or supra-exist them. (This raises questions of the effects of ideas and ideology, but Bourdieu doesn't write much or have much to say about ideology.) Sayer (2005), writing about the 'moral significance of class' and the attendant 'struggles of the social field', argues that Bourdieu's 'Pascalian' view of people as strategic, calculating actors leading lives largely determined by what is passed on to them culturally and that becomes a classed and gendered habitus, leads him to neglect the evaluative and ethical/moral drives in social life. Sayer uses some of the material and stories from 'The Weight of the World' (Bourdieu et al, 1999) and chapters such as 'Jonquil Street' to highlight that this moral evaluative dimension to social life is embedded in Bourdieu's own work, but not much dwelled upon by Bourdieu. Much as Bourdieu's insights and work are extremely valuable, I think Sayer's point and his attempt to modify and adapt Bourdieu's concept of habitus, extending it by adding a much stronger evaluative ethical dimension, is well made. Sayer argues that, despite his 'wickedly perceptive analysis of soft forms of domination' (Sayer, 2005, p 16), Bourdieu has little to say about the goods that people value, the commitments they have or the rationale, often ethical-care oriented, for the investments they make in other people or practices. Sayer argues that actors engage in practices not just for the advantage it will bring, or for strategic reasons, but because they are involved in moral–ethical struggles for the 'goods' of life in a broad sense, just as much as if not more than they are in strategic-advantage seeking action within particular fields. At a surface level the idea that we are conditioned to act in habitual ways has much to offer when trying to understand life in the Bridgetown Estate. There is indeed a good case to be made that action is habituated to class and gender positions based on the material and affective worlds that people find themselves in. One of the strongest such arguments would be based on the reproduction of life on the estate through and over generations. But Bourdieu's conception of the social world does not explain, for instance, the investments and commitments that people such as Rosy, Steph, Teresa or Michelle have to their children or to friends or family. There is more to life and social action on the Bridgetown Estate than just habituality, predispositions or inclinations. There is a constant daily struggle to survive, yes, but also to care and to love for those one is connected to. People are evaluative beings who are constantly weighing the world as it appears to them and the realities and limitations they confront. While they are involved in daily struggles to find work and food, the struggles of the social field that they engage in are also filled with investment and commitment and evaluative consciousness. As Rosy says quite often, "What will it be like when my child is older, what will I do then?" She is constantly assessing the nature of how life will be and should be as she goes through life. This is undoubtedly connected to the gendered nature of life on the estate, in that women undoubtedly have a much stronger and more developed ethic of care as to what is a good life for themselves and for their children. They do not want to 'stay in' or 'know their place'. They want better lives, even if the articulation is often incoherent. There is an ongoing struggle and tension between the culture of the group and their needs, wants and desires in life.

13

Class geography: part of no part

Time indeed is indifferent to us, but we are not indifferent to it, and
we are not indifferent to it because we move, for a duration, through
it, making and being made in it. In this our explanatory consciousness
of the past can inform our understanding of the present and illuminate
projects and strategies for a future, shaped but unmade. (Bhaskar,
2009, p 219)

In the last part of this extended conclusion, we will return to the place that
is the Bridgetown Estate that people move through over time, as suggested
by Bhaskar earlier, in order to understand the importance of place for the
residents, but also its relation to the larger (urban–national–global) space in
which it is embedded. As Sayer (1985, p 60) forcefully reminds us, 'Concrete
research must take spatial into account even if it is not directly interested in
it.' There are important things about the estate as place that I want to address
in this final chapter, and they include the following:

• The estate is simultaneously both part and no part of the geography
of a classed city. It is a place embedded in segregated urban space. The
ambiguous nature of the relationality between the part/whole estate/
city is crucial to this conclusion. This is connected to the fact that the
estate, and public housing in general, is mispresented through naming
and nomenclature and what passes for 'knowledge', that is, through the
use of terms and concepts such as 'deprived' or 'disadvantaged' or 'socially
excluded' as opposed to what I am arguing for here, which is the real of
classed and gendered places, spaces and cities.
• The estate has 'historicity' through time.
• The estate is a place of sensuous being and praxis.

These are conceptual distinctions, for in reality they form part of a totality
between local–city, part–whole, agency–culture structure (Archer, 1988)
and, not least in the last part of this final chapter, the phenomenology of
place. The totality that is place and space is constituted by this dialectic
or relationality. Just as there are relationalities of love and care, or those
embodied in paid work between workers and bosses, there are also those that
constitute the geographical and spatial dimensions of our lives. I take seriously
Sayer's (2000, pp 108–130) injunction that we must try to understand the
intersection of *time, space and process* and try not to engage in *spatial fetishism*

as he describes, whereby space takes on powers of its own without agency or people, as it were (Harvey, 1993, p 21). It is the relationship between time, space and social process that constitutes social reality, as it were. Places, just like things, have to be made, and remade, and perhaps even unmade as is happening in Bridgetown, and elsewhere in similar places. The nature of this connection between social relations and spatial structures (Gregory and Urry 1985; Thrift, 1996) is important and has been noted by many, and is perhaps the essence of much of geographical inquiry. As Edward Soja (1985, p 94) tells us, 'social life is materially constituted in its spatiality' in that the spatial is essentially constitutive of social reality and not just a background.

In other words, history and social reality are made and produced in specific geographical locations. Social relations and social history unfold somewhere, and not in an aspatial vacuum. But there are 'levels' to this reality that stretch from the most local places of interaction on the steps of the Bridgetown Estate to the surrounding environs, to the broader city, the nation-state and beyond. Woven into and through such geographies are sets of social relations that we have already described. If we start from the outside, as it were, and work our way back to the estate, the city reflects back in the built environment class structures physically objectified in space. Time is central to this, in that such landscape physics change over time. We can see and get a sense of this when we look at the nature and perception of the estate in its current manifestation whereby it has physically decayed to such an extent, due to purposeful neglect and lack of serious maintenance, that it needs to be fixed or replaced, thus altogether redrafting its original manifestation like so many other public housing estates (Romyn, 2016). When the estate was first built it was novel, even progressive for its time, but as the city and the world has changed and as it decayed physically it has thrown into relief even more starkly how such places reflect such (changing) social relations and class structures. As we have said already, it is ideology and distorted narratives such as those constructed on the notions of deprivation and disadvantage that obscure and mystify this by reifying and essentialising estates like Bridgetown.

Class, therefore, is materially constituted in this way in the neighbourhoods and buildings of the estate, the town, the city. Class has location and structure in space, of which the Bridgetown Estate is a concrete manifestation. If we apply such a reading of spatiality to the work undertaken here, the Bridgetown Estate is a spatial manifestation of the social relations that are Irish society. It is located in the lower reaches of what Henri Lefebvre described as 'a meticulous hierarchy of place' (Lefebvre, 1996, p 114). There is *class history* (Engels, 2009; Ranciere, 2012; O Carroll and Bennett, 2017), but there is also *class geography*, and they are intimately related. As Shildrick (2018) said earlier of the Grenfell Estate, the Bridgetown Estate is similarly a place that houses the working class. People located in similar positions and places in the social class structure are positioned and placed here together. The city council criteria for admission determines this class homogeneity in that one *must* be in the specified lower-income brackets to be eligible to be housed there. Such a critical social fact is often overlooked. And, as we have seen, this is an increasingly feminised working class. The estate is therefore a physical embodiment of the social class relations that characterise Irish society. This is the 'real' that underlies appearances and the mundane taken-for-granted everyday life. While 'space' is often used as a catch-all term that describes everything from the smallest locale to global, planetary and extra-planetary cosmic space, geographers and others make a useful conceptual distinction between 'place' and 'space' (Relph, 1985, pp 24–29; Harvey, 1993, p 4; Merryfield, 1993). Place is generally synonymous with the local, while space tends to be defined as something more general, beyond the local, sometimes described or defined as 'empty' or 'abstract' space, although there is a continuum or link that connects the two and builds a bridge between them, as it were (Massey, 1993; Urry, 2000; Harvey, 2011). Drawing on Marx's analysis of the circulation of capital as both a thing and a process, and comparing it with the wave-particle theory of quantum mechanics where atoms are simultaneously both (unperceived) wave and (perceived) particle, Merryfield (1993, p 522) tries to provide a unitary theory of place and space that can hold and understand local places and global 'flows' of space, or, as he puts it another way, 'things' and 'flows' within a dialectical theory of totality:

> place is not merely abstract space: it is the terrain where basic social practices – consumption, enjoyment, tradition, self-identification, solidarity, social support and social reproduction, etc. – are lived out. As a moment of capitalist space, place is where everyday life is situated. And as such, place can be taken as practiced space.

Perhaps the important thing here is the dialectic between something fixed in place with movement(s) in space that changes both, over time. This is what Merryfield (1993, p 521) calls the 'thing and flow nature of reality'. Such currents of change flow through the thing that is the Bridgetown Estate. Therefore, just as social relations have ontological depth, so too do spatial relations. Not only is the totality socially stratified but it is also at the same time spatially stratified. The two are inherently related. If the *real* nature of social relations is difficult to discern and understand, it is perhaps all the more odd that the physical partitioning of groups and classes that is visible to the eye should be even more so. Using this simplified conceptual analogy, the Bridgetown Estate is simultaneously a place, while also being part of larger, extended space. The dialectic between place and space, as I suggested at the beginning of this chapter, is in reality indivisible and forms a totality. If we add all of the local places together, they make up the totality of space in the larger sense. They are simultaneously the one and the many (Merryfield, 1993, pp 520–521).

My point here is that the Bridgetown Estate is both local place and at the same time connected to the larger space of the city and the nation-state and beyond. But this spatial relationship takes a very particular form, in that the estate in a number of important ways occupies a subordinate, exploited position within this totality. This is not to say that the estate is not also a place of possibility and potentiality, for it clearly is. This place–space or local–city, estate–global relation (O Byrne, 1997, pp 73–89) expresses itself in different ways, whether it is in the sphere of work and the economy whereby the estate becomes functional for the city as a 'growth machine' for the accumulation of capital, as it has been called; or in a different sense there is something that implicitly says to people 'know your place' (Connolly, 2017) in this socio-geography that striates the city with grids and distinction lines, but that does not exist on any maps as such. Such tracks and routes and pathways are *implicit*. The two are connected, in that while the city is a production site for the economics of class it is also a site for the playing out of distinction where, for almost all of the time spent with people from the estate, they rarely mix or cross class boundaries beyond the necessary relations they must engage in for work, for example, or in the crossover consumption zones of the city core. That is, only when they must, or with permission from the more powerful. Boundaries may be transgressed, but it is usually temporary. Cultural distinctions are embodied in the physics of the city. Class boundaries, while generally implicit, remain clearly demarcated, and one must know one's place not alone in the social and economic hierarchy, but also in the spatial landscape. Such understandings and knowledge of how to use the city and of where to go and not to go are deeply embedded in people's practices and consciousness.

To borrow and modify slightly a concept from Jacques Ranciere (1999), the estate is simultaneously both 'part and no part' of the 'space' of a classed city. As a constituent part of a social totality, it is similar and different, it belongs and doesn't belong, it is isotopic and heterotopic at the same time. Ranciere, describing the three major classes that made up the Athenian polis, the wealthy *Oligoi*, the virtuous *Arete* and the *Demos* of ordinary Athenians, tells us, following Aristotle, that it is the Demos who are the part of no part, the count of the uncounted (Ranciere, 1999, p 90) in the Athenian city-state. Like the inhabitants of Plato's cave, their lives are characterised by forms of unconscious slavery mistakenly understood as freedom. The Demos, as the largest of the three classes that constitute the core of the social structure of the Athenian city-state, stands in an ambiguous relationship to the whole, in that it appears to belong but does not in reality belong. All ancient Athenian politics is geared toward concealing, justifying and managing this fact that the one and the many are not a coherent unity. Despite the beauty and philosophical inquiry of the Athenian polis there are those who have no part, and it is a place where slavery, class and patriarchy are each integral to the functioning of city life and the city-state. The Greek polis or city-state needs those who work so that those who want to think and make rhetoric can do so.

Distinctions today may be a little more fuzzy, but the Bridgetown Estate has a similar paradoxical and ambiguous relationship with the city and state in that it has *Dasein* or thereness (Heidegger) or extension (Spinoza) in the here and now and stands on a piece of earth and is visible from all sides and above. The estate has girth and presence on the landscape. And yet, if one listens or looks closely, the estate speaks and manifests in its very physical being an implicit *dispute* (Ranciere, 1999, p 100) over how class segregation is built into the physical fabric of the city. The spoken phrase *it's not where you live, it's how you live*, is in a real sense an acknowledgment that one must prove that one can belong, but the nagging feeling remains that one will never belong. In this sense the estate is connected in a functional sense and yet remains in many moral–ethical–political senses separate from the larger body of the city as a site with particular class characteristics. It is simultaneously part and no-part of the palimpsest of the city.

This ambiguity takes different forms, in that the estate's relation with the larger space works undoubtedly at an economic level in that it is viewed and utilised as a pragmatic utilitarian resource or pool of labour power to be exploited. For all of its existence, the estate and its inhabitants have had an ambivalent and antagonistic relationship with the various industrial and post-industrial forms of capitalism that have existed in the spaces that surround and environ it. Capital flows have come and gone and come back again, albeit for different reasons and in different forms. Capital has invested and disinvested. It has made and unmade the areas surrounding the estate and now wants to remake them anew. It has put down roots for a while and then pulled them up and left for cheaper labour pools. If it couldn't move and remained rooted to place, it rationalised, technologised and slimmed and trimmed and reduced dramatically the need for labour. Sources of nutrition were turned on and off and metamorphosed over time from one form to another, such as the changes from industry to retail and to services. Slews of factories appeared and then disappeared over decades as the waterholes of work that surrounded the estate dried up, leaving drought and famine for long periods. Hospitals, state agencies and supermarkets became replacement sources of employment. Such changes over time bring to light what Heidegger (2003, p 401) called 'the temporality of being-in-the-world.' Austerity sharpened the neoliberal blade that was wielded with particular verve and that highlighted the active role of 'the state as a stratifying and classifying agency', a 'centaur state' that is, according to Wacquant (2019, pp 39–42), liberal and rewarding for those at the top while disciplinary and punitive for those at the bottom. It is quite possible that similar retrenchment of the welfare state will occur in a post-COVID world. Like many public housing estates and projects described in other works (Wacquant, 2008; Rogaly and Taylor, 2011; Hanley, 2012; McKenzie, 2015; Rosbrook Thompson and Armstrong, 2018; Watt, 2021), from its first days the estate was connected in various ways to the capitalist economy through the space of the city and beyond. Many of the disused textile, food and machine factories where estate residents like Nadia once worked have recently become sites for renewed capital investment that is repurposing them for the private rental housing market or rented student accommodation. It is important to say at this point that I am not arguing for, nor do I think that residents of the estate have a nostalgia for, a golden age when they were effectively 'satisfied with being dissatisfied' (Gibson Graham, 2006, p 13). Charlie's life or Rosy's or Frank's are good examples of the feeling of not realising one's true nature and how it hangs heavy on the heart and the psyche. I think they would prefer another world altogether. The important point is that there have been significant qualitative changes in their worlds over decades.

The search for new outlets for expansion and accumulation, however, does not only take place in the working spaces surrounding the estate. For the *inherited space* of the estate is itself a potential *projected space* (Lipietz in Soja, 1985, p 118), in that there are also additional ways to extract surplus value than through labour alone. As has been clearly the case with other such estates in the city, the land on which the estate stands may well prove to be its most exploitable and irresistible resource. And, while it hasn't been central to this work as such, there has been and is currently a highly active capitalist logic that says while it might have been the practice in the past and present for working-class people to live and to be housed in such places, this no longer holds, and such sites hold untapped potential for capital extraction and value, usually in the form of rent. This reflects the contingency of what we understand as public housing and how its nature and form and relation to the whole, as it were, have changed over time. We are witnessing a significant change in the city landscape, or, as Lefebvre (1996, p 107) put it in more trans-historical terms, 'Each urban formation knew an ascent, an apogee, a decline.' But this is not natural decline, it is a manufactured one. As I and others have written about previously (Bissett, 2008; Hearne, 2011), public housing tenants have discovered more and more that the places where they live can easily be taken from them. 'Accumulation by dispossession' (Harvey, 2013; Lees and White, 2020), as has already happened in many other city council estates, is also a very real possibility here.

Lefebvre's theoretical triad of *perceived*, *conceived* and *lived* outlined in *The Production of Space* (Lefebvre, 1991, pp 38–39) is a useful tool in such a context to understand how urban space is produced and its different aspects or components. In particular, the triad offers a bridge from the physical–perceptual, to conceptual–spatial level, to local–cultural–anthropological world. These concepts correspond roughly to the *physical*, *mental* and *social* nature or characteristics of space, and in this triad there is an interpenetration and relationality between the inanimate structures of the natural-physical world, the abstract structures of space and place as conceived in the mind and the everyday lived anthropological cultural world of practices and customs in-place. As Zeleniac (2018, p 7), writing on Lefebvre and the triad, puts it, 'Space is produced in a dynamic relationship between all three parts. There is thus a reciprocal relationship between the elements involved in its production.' *Spatial practice* in Lefebvre's schema corresponds to the physical nature of the rural, the town or the city. Such spatial practice produces what we see or *perceive* in the buildings and monuments of the city or the rural estate of the Latifundia of landlords and peasants in medieval Italy, for example, which was defined with particular precision and characteristics as to how and where the respective classes would live. Spatial practice and the perceived are coterminous for Lefebvre. The physical nature of space and what exists within it often clearly reflect class relations and power structures in that, for example, the buildings and monuments of the wealthy reflect their wealth, while those of the working-class tell a different story, usually of the struggles and scarcities of class life. The Bridgetown Estate came into being, therefore, as part of the *spatial practice* that provided the buildings for housing the working-class and the propertyless in the city.

As for the second aspect of the triad, the Bridgetown Estate was *conceived* in the abstract before it became a particular urban form. Those who conceived the estate had very particular ideas and views about how people could or would live on the urban landscape, down to the precision and uniformity of space within and without each flat or housing unit. Public housing estates such as Bridgetown were therefore products of modernity and coincide with what is described and considered as an emerging *modern Ireland* or *modernity*, often written about from a historical and literary perspective (Kiberd, 1996; Ferriter, 2005; McCabe, 2013), but here as materialised in an urban context, although they are rarely if ever part of that official modernist history. They perhaps also belonged at their inception to the period described by Bauman (2012) as *heavy* or *solid modernity*, as opposed to the *light modernity* of post-industrial capitalism. The Bridgetown Estate was just one of many such estates built in mid-20th-century Ireland, many of them in Dublin. And, as we have seen, it is now being *reconceived* in the present under a different set of rules and ideas and with different priorities from when it was first conceived. This (re)conceiving is tied to interests and power. There is little to suggest that residents have any role in this reconceiving and they are kept largely at arm's length from decisions and actions about the estate's future. The place is currently a half-formed thing caught somewhere between what it was and what it will be or will no longer be. To borrow from Hegel's Logic, it is in a process of negation between being, nothing and becoming. Like so many other failed or stalled housing projects both here and elsewhere (Romyn, 2016; Watt, 2021), the estate may remain in this in-between liminal state for some time, and its new form and conception will undoubtedly have a relationship with larger economic forces seeking to colonise and acquire the land for returns on capital. Spatial practice is once again at work, and this highlights in Ozymandian fashion the temporal nature of places in time and space and the struggles as to what they will become or whether they will continue to exist in any recognisable form. New spatial practices, new abstractions and new interests may well deem it to be the case that there is no place for the working-class on such sites, due to those sites' value for Capital. There is clear evidence that such forces are at play in the city and country at large (Hearne, 2020).

The third part of Lefebvre's triad, and the one I will finish with here, refers to the socio-cultural everyday world and the fact that the people who came to live there subsequently took what had been conceived in the mind and then built through spatial practice and made it their 'lived' space and social world. Harvey (1993, pp 17–19) makes just such a point about Times Square and how it was transformed and recolonised by ordinary New Yorkers in a struggle against the desires of the rich and the powerful who conceived it exclusively for themselves. Places that are conceived by the rich for the rich may be recolonised, as it were, by ordinary people. There was a time when the Bridgetown Estate did not exist. It moved from conceptual form to physical reality, and then to inhabited social world. At one point while doing this research project I was given a black-and-white photograph of a group of workers standing in work overalls posing for the photo as the unfinished estate comes into being behind them. The photo shows the 'geo-historical earthing' (Sayer, 2000, p 135; Bhaskar, 2009, p 212) of the estate as it comes into being quite literally out of the earth from the labour of those who built it, some of whom subsequently came to live in this new estate. The labour of the dead is congealed in the bricks and mortar of an estate that was built to house the working-class poor of Dublin in new housing forms. This was to give them relief from the overcrowding and struggles of tenement living and other dilapidated forms of housing in the city. It was one of many such estates that came into being on the terrain of the city in the 20th century as also happened across much of mainland post-war Europe (Castells, 1983; Power, 1999; Brady, 2016, 2022). The nature of the estate is particular and is therefore a secretion of a particular historical period. Temporally, four to five generations have now passed through the estate, and perhaps it can also be said that the estate has passed through them, in that it has left an indelible imprint and trace on them. Residents have used it and continue to use it as a public resource and value as time has flowed. Even while it has physically deteriorated, reflecting its transitoriness and the fact that places, just like social structures, may be only relatively enduring, the estate has provided and retains significant use value and more for thousands of people in this regard. It has functioned in many ways as a 'commons', but the opposite is also a possibility, in that the estate (or a large portion of it) potentially faces a reconceptualisation that would move it away from a common public resource and requisition it in the interests of capital.

To use Lefebvre's (2014) well-known phrase, the estate is a quintessential site of *everyday life*. It is, as the phenomenologists say, a blend of matter and consciousness where being, time and place are riveted together (Charlesworth, 2000). What exist here are 'organic relations between subject and space, the gearing of the subject into his world that is the origin of space' (Merleau Ponty, 2012, p 262). Or, to say it differently, social space is animated and brought to life by social practice. Place functions as the location of the ludic and loric, of play and story, and is deeply emotional (Bachelard, 2014); and yet, as we have seen, it can also be a site of risk and harm to body and mind. Life must happen and be rooted somewhere, and place is often conceived as the location of sets of relationships built on emotional ties and solidary attachments, whereas space is conceived in more impersonal and abstract ways, though no less causally influential for that. Place, as Heidegger says, is where 'equipment' is 'ready to hand', where we are 'situated' actors carrying out or doing situated practices (Thrift, 1996; De Certeau, 2004). Residents often say that 'you can take the person out of Bridgetown but you can't take Bridgetown out of the person', as if the place were, like others have said of class (Kuhn, 1995; Moran, 2013; Cruz, 2021), something that gets under, and stays under, the skin. In some sense it is and does, and becomes part of one's being through happenings and events, use and play. The estate is a place of play and jouissance, especially for children. It is also full of memories and forgettings of the living and the dead and of the good and the bad. The dead are everywhere in images and in story. Death is the constant reminder, as Bhaskar says, that 'only relations endure'. Or, in Jean Luc Nancy's (1991, p 18) Heideggerian phrase, 'The being of the finite being exposes it to the end of Being.' In this sense the estate simultaneously is full of pres-ence and abs-ence or, to put it another way, it is permeated with life and death, the living live with their dead (Ricoeur, 2004, 2016). From stories of estate women acting as midwives to each other, bringing new life to the estate while waiting on doctors who often never came, to the laying out of the dead in family flats or to the scar tissue of heroin, these things are redolent of the existential nature of life on the estate. This is what Heidegger's (1969) sense of *dwelling* or *locus of being* means when we transfer it to a public housing estate. [see also Seamon and Mugerauer, 1985] But there is no idealised state of Black Forest farmhouse bliss to return to. Life is hard and is tethered to capitalist modernity, and there is no going back, as it were, to a Yeatsian life in the '*bee loud glade*'. Individuals may retreat to the bucolic idyll, but change at the macro level of class will involve the ongoing development of 'a post-capitalist politics', at a collective level and not just at that of personal revelation. (Harvey, 1993; Gibson Graham, 2006; Dean, 2018). There is no nostalgia here for an archaic golden age or lost community. In this phenomenal sense, then, the Bridgetown Estate, in-itself, is a place-of-being-in-common-with-others-in-similar-class-conditions. For Jean Luc Nancy, 'being-in-common' is not an add-on to 'being-self' but is, rather 'co-originary and coextensive with it' (Luc Nancy, 1991, p xxxvii).

The estate is, therefore, a 'world' unto itself with all that that entails. It is encapsulated in the utterly plagiarised song that kids sing with lung-busting, bone-shaking vigour on summer project trips: 'We're from Bridgetown. The mighty mighty Bridgetown'. (It is always *We*.) Within their own orbit the residents of the Bridgetown Estate remain autochthonous beings who are rooted in place. At a primitive level the estate is a place of shelter and sustenance, even if it is wrought with fragility. Family histories reach back into the past, and there is the present of one's own children and friends. There are sinewy webs of attachment (Inglis, 2014) to kin and to others on the estate. As we have seen, these extend out into the inner and outer working-class neighbourhoods of the city as children married and left to start new lives in estates near and far (Young and Wilmott, 1957; Brody, 1973; Rogaly and Taylor, 2011). For residents such as Rosy, Michelle, Nadia or Frank, their being-ness is wrapped tightly with that of the estate. It has a social and cultural existence in and of itself that runs and flows through time made manifest in what they say and do and in the stories they tell. Rosy can recall with precise detail the emotional resonance of her mother's sudden death in the old family flat and the trauma it entailed. She can describe with similar precision, and does a good impression of, her late next-door neighbour with a lisp and an immaculate dress sense and the regular trip to the off-licence for the Powers whiskey that she went there to buy for him. This being-in-common-with-others becomes being-in-common-with-others-in-this-place and the tactile relationship between residents and the physical fabric of the estate and the uses it is put to by people, whether it be the interior of a home filled with the mementos of a life or the sensuous points of connection and social exchange such as the steps or hallways or the observatories that are the balconies, in what has been described as a 'motor and neural interface between self and world' (Gibson Graham, 2006, p 127; Hanley, 2012). What Hagerstrand (1967) called 'stations', and Giddens (1985) 'regions', are the stopping points like the steps where social life flares up, catching fire, and then dies out in daily rhythm. The estate is 'embodied' by residents in that they animate it with their bodies, thereby animating the matter of the estate. They infuse it with life. This reciprocity fills the back and front spaces of the estate and the points of contact and encounters where social life is generated and sustained. Such recesses and nodes produce what Bachelard (2014) calls a 'poetics of space' that is sometimes beyond language or even pre-conscious or pre-reflective doings as to how beings occupy places. Moving within or away from the estate often jolted such senses to life. On one occasion, as she was in the process of moving from her flat, a woman stood mute and immobile after she discovered, for the first time, jottings and writings that her father had left concealed in a small, smooth, wooden box about his life as a young man going back and forward to England to find paid work.

Journeys and motion bring residents out into the intermediate space beyond the estate and into the core of the city itself. The estate may be a world unto itself, but it is not an island, and the nature of this relationship between part and whole also has a phenomenological dimension and use. The relationship to and the use of the city is conditioned and manifests itself in particular ways, one of which is the organic knowledge and use of streets and landscapes. People know where they should and should not be and where they can or cannot be, even if such knowledge is not totally conscious. Rosy's child is being engeographied to the streets of the neighbourhood and beyond as we walk. In Ulyssean fashion the child learns the streets, so to speak. Having wandered and walked a lot with people in the surrounding environs of the estate, to a large degree people have psychic maps as to how to use and how to navigate from the estate into the surrounding areas and the city. If Bloom navigated the city for lemon soap, a gorgonzola sandwich or erotica, for Rosy, Steph and Charlie their circumambulations are more likely to be for basic necessities, even if they too occasionally wander aimlessly and forget themselves like Bloom. It is not insular nationalists they fear, so much as hunger. Yet, there is much repetition in the coming and the going, whether it is to the shops, to seek out food, to other similar estates, to clinics or the community café. Unless it is necessary for paid work, or they are being taken on a trip, for instance, people rarely stray from the *class tracks and zones* that have been laid down previously. They live lives within a particular geographical world and the city has its own way of telling them do not come here unless, for instance, you have money to spend, which they usually do not. And they do not go there. The walking tracks and the journeys people take therefore follow implicit class lines of the city. Like the women in Skeggs's study (2002) who are made to feel out of place in a luxury goods shop, Rosy's antennae perking up at a funeral in a city centre church displays a similar sense of being or feeling out of place. 'There are lots of nice people here', is her way of saying that they are different to her, and she is in the *wrong* place or is *out of place*. She knows her own people and they are back in her own place, and she needs to get back there.

Conclusion: absenting absences, ills and constraints

Transcendental critical realism is a normative social philosophy. It takes a position that says that if we can identify and remove avoidable sources of suffering, we should strive to do so. Bads or ills that affect us as a species can and should be eliminated. This work has shown that there are many constraints, ills and absences that work to constrain and limit the lives of the people living on the Bridgetown Estate. These are unfulfilled needs, wants and desires. They are goods in the broad sense. Such constraints produce and add to various forms of alienation. They prohibit flourishing and self-realisation and the possibility of a society based on eudamonia where the flourishing of each is a condition for the flourishing of all. I agree with Bhaskar and the many of those working from the perspective of critical social science that our task is to absent such absences, and to remove such ills and constraints that prohibit a true realisation of being and life; the ills produced by the classic alienation of separation from the tasks and products of one's labour, of one's species being where what one produces takes on a life of its own and one is subject to the class relations of capitalism. The materiality of class, despite the shift to more cultural forms of analysis, has not disappeared as many would contend. There are other constraints, such as those that emerge from or are the product of the scarcity and absence of resources such as food or money. We are a long way from universal human flourishing or the eudaimonistic society, but that is what we must strive for. This is the alethic truth that we must reach (Bhaskar, 2008b, p 282). This book raises many questions, especially for change. I have tried in this conclusion to emphasise the importance and relations between class, gender and place to the objects that are public housing estates. I have begun to develop a realist theory that takes into account not just the experience and the events that mark lives but also describes and explains the effects that larger processes and structures have on such estates. This is the domain of the real, where structures are visible only in their effects. Much previous work has focused on effects, but has done little to understand or to explain the mechanisms that are producing such effects. This stratified realist view of the social world of a public housing estate, I would argue, brings us to a clearer understanding, even if we constantly have to reassess things as they change. And if we return to and conclude with Ranciere's concept of the demos, there is always a vibration of hope: 'Wherever the part of no part is inscribed, however fragile and fleeting these inscriptions may be, a sphere of the demos is created, an element of the *kratos*, the power of the people exists. The problem is to extend the sphere of this materialization, to maximize its power' (Ranciere, 1999, p 88).

References

Adair, V. (2002) 'Branded with Infamy: Inscriptions of Poverty and Class in the United States', *Signs*, 27(2): 451–471.

Ahmed, S. (2008) 'Sociable Happiness', *Emotion Space and Society*, 1(1): 10–13.

Allen, K. (2012) 'The Model Pupil Who Faked the Test: Social Policy in the Irish Crisis', *Critical Social Policy*, 32(3): 422–439.

Allen, K. with B.O. Boyle (2013) *Austerity Ireland: The Failure of Irish Capitalism.* Pluto Press.

Archer, M. (1988) *Culture and Agency: The Place of Culture in Social Theory.* Cambridge University Press.

Archer, M. (2000) *Being Human: The Problem of Agency.* Cambridge University Press.

Archer, M., Bhaskar, R., Collier, A., Lawson, T. and Norrie, A. (1998) *Critical Realism: Essential Readings.* Centre for Critical Realism. Routledge.

Aristotle (2004) *The Nicomachean Ethics.* Penguin Classics.

Atkinson, W. (2015) *Class.* Polity Press.

Bachelard, G. (2014) *The Poetics of Space.* Penguin Books.

Baker, J., Lynch, K., Cantillon, S. and Walsh, J. (2004) *Equality: From Theory to Action.* Palgrave Macmillan.

Ball, E. (2019) 'Exploring Family-Based Intervention Mechanisms as a Form of Statecraft', in J. Flint and R. Powell (eds) *Class, Ethnicity and State in the Polarized Metropolis: Putting Wacquant to Work.* Palgrave Macmillan, pp 107–134.

Bauman, Z. (2012) *Liquid Modernity.* Polity Press.

Bhaskar, R. (2008a) *A Realist Theory of Science.* Verso.

Bhaskar, R. (2008b) *Dialectic: The Pulse of Freedom.* Routledge.

Bhaskar, R. (2009) *Scientific Realism and Human Emancipation.* Routledge.

Bhaskar, R. (2015) *The Possibility of Naturalism.* Routledge.

Bissett, J. (2008) *Regeneration: Public Good or Private Profit.* Tasc at New Island Books.

Bissett, J. (2015) 'Defiance and Hope: Austerity and the Community Sector in the Republic of Ireland', in C. Coulter and A. Nagle (eds) *Ireland Under Austerity: Neoliberal Crisis, Neoliberal Solutions.* Manchester University Press, pp 171–191.

Blokland, T. (2008) '"You Got to Remember You Live in Public Housing": Place Making in an American Housing Project', *Housing, Theory and Society*, 25(1): 31–46.

Blokland, T. (2019) '"We Live like Prisoners in a Camp": Surveillance, Governance and Agency in a US Housing Project', in J. Flint and R. Powell (eds) *Class, Ethnicity and State in the Polarized Metropolis: Putting Wacquant to Work.* Palgrave Macmillan, pp 53–80.

References

Boltanski, L. and Chiapello, E. (2005) 'The New Spirit of Capitalism', *The International Journal of Politics Culture and Society*, 18: 161–188.

Bourdieu, P. (1977) *Outline of a Theory of Practice*. Cambridge University Press.

Bourdieu, P. (1986) 'The Forms of Capital' in J. Richardson (ed) *Handbook of Theory and Research for the Sociology of Education*. Greenwood Press, pp 241–258.

Bourdieu, P. (1987) 'What Makes a Social Class? On the Theoretical and Practical Existence of Groups', *Berkeley Journal of Sociology*, 32: 1–17.

Bourdieu, P. (1989) 'Social Space and Symbolic Power', *Sociological Theory*, 7(1): 14–25.

Bourdieu, P. (1991) *Language and Symbolic Power*. Polity Press.

Bourdieu, P. (1993) *The Field of Cultural Production*. Columbia University Press.

Bourdieu, P. (2000) *Distinction: A Social Critique of the Judgement of Taste*. Routledge.

Bourdieu, P. and Wacquant, L. (1992) *Invitation to a Reflexive Sociology*. Polity Press.

Bourdieu, P., Accardo, A., Balzas, G., Beaud, S., Bonvin, F., et al (1999) *The Weight of the World: Social Suffering in Contemporary France*. Polity Press.

Brady, J. (2016) *Dublin, 1950–1970: Houses, Flats and High Rise*. Four Courts Press.

Brady, J. (2022) *Dublin from 1970 to 1990: The City Transformed*. Four Courts Press.

Brody, H. (1973) *Inishkillane: Change and Decline in the West of Ireland*. Allen Lane.

Brown, W. (2015) *Undoing the Demos: Neoliberalism's Stealth Revolution*. Zone Books.

Caplan, C. (2004) 'The Death of the Working Class Hero', *New Formations*, 52 (Spring): 94–110.

Castells, M. (1983) *The City and the Grassroots: A Cross Cultural Theory of Urban Social Movements*. University of California Press.

Charlesworth, S. (2000) *A Phenomenology of Working Class Experience*. Cambridge University Press.

Coles, R. and Haro, L. (2019) 'Toward a Democratic Groove', *Angelaki Journal of the Theoretical Humanities*, 24(4): 103–119.

Collier, A. (1994) *Critical Realism: An Introduction to Roy Bhaskar's Philosophy*. Verso.

Connell, R.W. (2018) *Masculinities*, 2nd edn. Polity Press.

Connolly, N. (2017) *Know Your Place: Essays on the Working Class by the Working Class*. Dead Ink.

Coulter, C. (1999) *Contemporary Northern Irish Society: An Introduction*. Pluto Press.

Coulter, C. and Nagle, A. (2015) *Ireland under Austerity: Neoliberal Crisis, Neoliberal Solutions.* Manchester University Press.

Crean, M. (2018) 'Affective Formations of Class Consciousness: Care Consciousness', *The Sociological Review*, 66(6): 1177–1193.

Croghan, A. (2014) *Wildchild.* Penguin Books.

Cruz, C. (2021) *The Melancholia of Class: A Manifesto for the Working Class.* Repeater Books.

Dalla Costa, M. (1995) 'Capitalism and Reproduction', in W. Bonefeld, R. Gunn, J. Holloway and K. Psychopedis (eds) *Open Marxism, Volume 3.* Pluto Press.

Dean, J. (2018) *The Communist Horizon.* Verso.

De Certeau, M. (2004) *The Practice of Everyday Life.* University of California Press.

De Cocteau, C.L. (2012) 'The Art of Ethnography', *Journal for the Theory of Social Behaviour*, 47(1): 58–82.

Dorling, D. (2015) *Injustice: Why Social Inequality Still Persists.* Policy Press.

Eagleton, T. (2010) *On Evil.* Yale University Press.

Elster, J. (1982) 'Beliefs, Bias and Ideology', in M. Hollis and S. Lukes (eds) *Rationality and Relativism.* Basil Blackwater Publisher Limited, pp 123–148.

Emecheta, B. (2018) *In The Ditch.* An Ogwugwu Afor Book.

Engels, F. (2009) *The Condition of the Working Class in England.* Oxford University Press.

Fahey, T. et al. (1999) *Social Housing in Ireland. A Study of Success, Failure and Lessons Learned.* Oak Tree Press in Association with the Katherine Howard Foundation. Combat Poverty Agency.

Fanstein, S. (1996) 'Justice, Politics and the Creation of Urban Space', in *The Urbanization of Injustice.* Lawrence and Wishart, pp 18–44.

Fay, B. (1987) *Critical Social Science: Liberation and its Limits.* Cornell University Press.

Federici, S. (2010) 'The Reproduction of Labour Power in the Global Economy: Marxist Theory and the Unfinished Feminist Revolution', *Globalizations*, 3.

Ferguson, S. (2020) *Women and Work: Feminism, Labour, and Social Reproduction.* Pluto Press.

Ferriter, D. (2005) *The Transformation of Modern Ireland.* The Overlook Press.

Folbre, N. and Hartmann, H. (1989) 'The rhetoric of self-interest: Ideology of gender in economic theory', in *The Consequences of Economic Rhetoric.* Cambridge University Press, pp 184–204.

Foucault, M. (1991) *Discipline and Punish: The Birth of the Prison.* Penguin Books.

Fraser, N. and Honneth, A. (2003) *Redistribution or Recognition: A Political Philosophical Exchange.* Verso.

Fraser, S. (2018) *Class Matters: The Strange Career of an American Delusion.* Yale University Press.

Friedman, S. and Laurison, D. (2020) *The Class Ceiling: Why It Pays to Be Privileged.* Policy Press.

Garthwaite, K. (2016) *Hunger Pains: Life inside Foodbank Britain.* Policy Press.

Geertz, C. (2017) *The Interpretation of Cultures: Selected Essays.* Foreword by Robert Darnton. Basic Books.

Gibson Graham, J.K. (2006) *A Postcapitalist Politics.* University of Minnesota Press.

Giddens, A. (1985) 'Time, Space and Regionalisation', in D. Gregory and J. Urry (eds) *Social Relations and Spatial Structures: Critical Human Geography.* Macmillan, pp 265–295.

Gilligan, C. (1982) *In a Different Voice: Psychological Theory and Women's Development.* Harvard University Press.

Glucksmann, M. (aka Ruth Cavendish) (1982) *Women on the Line: From Experience to Reflection: Changes and Continuities in Women's Work.* Routledge.

Gouldner, A. (1962) 'Anti-Minotaur: The Myth of a Value Free Sociology', *Social Problems*, 9(3): 199–213.

Graeber, D. (2011) *Debt: The First 5000 Years.* Melville House Publishing.

Gramsci, A. (2005) *Selections from the Prison Notebooks.* Lawrence and Wishart.

Gregory, D. and Urry, J. (1985) *Social Relations and Spatial Structures. Critical Human Geography.* Macmillan.

Hagerstrand, T. (1967) *Innovation Diffusion as a Spatial Process.* University of Chicago Press.

Hall, S., Massey, D. and Rustin, M. (2011) *After Neoliberalism? The Kilburn Manifesto.* Soundings.

Hanley, L. (2012) *Estates: An Intimate History.* Granta.

Hanlon, N. (2012) *Masculinities, Care and Equality: Identity and Nurture in Men's Lives.* Palgrave Macmillan.

Harvey, D. (1993) 'From Space to Place and Back Again: Reflections on the Condition of Postmodernity', in J. Bird., B. Curtis, T. Putnam, G. Robertson and L. Tuckner (eds) *Mapping the Futures: Local Cultures, Global Change.* Routledge.

Harvey, D. (2005) *A Brief History of Neoliberalism.* Oxford University Press.

Harvey, D. (2009) *Social Justice and the City*, rev edn, Geographies of Justice and Social Transformation. University of Georgia Press.

Harvey, D. (2011) *The Enigma of Capital and the Crises of Capitalism.* Profile Books.

Harvey, D. (2013) *The New Imperialism.* Oxford University Press.

Hearne, R. (2011) *Public Private Partnerships in Ireland: Failed Experiment or the Way Forward?* Manchester University Press.

Hearne, R. (2020) *Housing Shock: The Irish Housing Crisis and How to Solve It*. Policy Press.

Hegel, G.W.F. (1977) *Phenomenology of Spirit*. Oxford University Press.

Heidegger, M. (1969) *Discourse on Thinking: A Translation of Gelassenheit*. Translated by J. Anderson and E. Hans Freund. Harper and Row Publishers.

Heidegger, M. (2003) *Being and Time*. Blackwell.

Hochschild, A.R. (1983) *The Managed Heart: Commercialisation of Human Feeling*. University of California Press.

Hochschild, A.R. (1997) *The Time Bind: When Work Becomes Home and Home Becomes Work*. Holt Paperbacks.

Hoggart, R. (1957) *The Uses of Literacy: Aspects of Working Class Life with Special References to Publications and Entertainments*. Trent University.

hooks, b. (2000) *Where We Stand: Class Matters*. Routledge.

Hourigan, N. (2011) *Understanding Limerick: Social Exclusion and Change*. Cork University Press.

Inglis, T. (2014) *Meanings of Life in Contemporary Ireland: Webs of Significance*. Palgrave Macmillan.

Jenkins, R. (2002) *Pierre Bourdieu*, rev edn, Key Sociologist Series. Routledge.

Jones, O. (2012) *Chavs: The Demonization of the Working Class*. Verso.

Kelleher, P. and O Neill, C. (2018) *The Systematic Destruction of the Community Development, Anti-poverty and Equality Movement 2002–2015*. Kelleher Associates.

Kiberd, D. (1996) *Inventing Ireland: The Literature of the Modern Nation*. Vintage Books.

Kittay, E. (1999) *Love's Labour*. Routledge.

Kuhn, A. (1995) *Family Secrets: Acts of Memory and Imagination*. Verso.

Lees, L. and White, H. (2020) 'The Social Cleansing of London Council Estates: Everyday Experiences of Accumulative Dispossession'. *Housing Studies*, 35(10): 1701–1722.

Lefebvre. H. (1991) *The Production of Space*. Blackwell Publishing.

Lefebvre, H. (1996) 'The Right to the City' in *Writings on Cities*. Translated and edited by E. Kofman and E. Lebas. Blackwell Publishers.

Lefebvre, H. (2014) *Critique of Everyday Life: The One Volume Edition*. Verso. First published as *Critique de la Vie Quotidienne: L'introduction* (1947).

Louis, E. (2017) *The End of Eddie*. Harvill Secker.

Luc Nancy, J. (1991) *The Inoperative Community*. Theory and History of Literature vol 76, edited by P. Connor. University of Minnesota Press.

Lynch, K. (2022) *Care and Capitalism: Why Affective Equality Matters for Social Justice*. Polity Press.

Lynch, K., Baker, J. and Lyons, M. (2009) *Affective Equality: Love, Care and Injustice*. Palgrave Macmillan.

Lynch, K. and Kalaitzake, M. (2020) 'Affective and Calculative Solidarity: The Impact of Individualism and Neoliberal Capitalism', *European Journal of Social Theory*, 23(2): 238–257.

Lynch, K. and O Neill, C. (1994) 'The Colonisation of Social Class in Education', *British Journal of Sociology of Education*, 15(3): 307–324.

Mahony, P. and Zmroczek, C. (1997) *Class Matters: 'Working-Class' Women's Perspectives on Social Class*. Taylor & Francis.

Marsh, B. (2020) *The Logic of Violence: An Ethnography of Dublin's Illegal Drug Trade*. Routledge.

Marx, K. (1993) *Grundrisse. Foundations of the Critique of Political Economy*. Penguin Classics in association with New Left Review.

Massey, D. (1993) 'Power geometry and a progressive sense of place', in J. Bird, B. Curtis, T. Putnam, G. Robertson and L. Tuckner (eds) *Mapping the Futures: Local Cultures, Global Change*. Routledge, pp 59–69.

Mau, S. (2015) *Inequality, Marketization and the Majority Class: Why did the European Middle Class accept Neoliberalism?* Palgrave Macmillan.

Mauss, M. (1990) *The Gift: The Form and Reason for Exchange in Archaic Societies*. Routledge.

McCabe, C. (2013) *Sins of the Father: Decisions that Shaped the Irish Economy*. The History Press Ireland.

McGarvey, D. (2018) *Poverty Safari*. Picador.

McIntyre, A. (2007) *After Virtue: A Study in Moral Theory*. University of Notre Dame Press.

McKenzie, L. (2015) *Getting By: Estates, Class and Culture in Austerity Britain*. Policy Press.

Mellor, M. (2010) *The Future of Money: From Financial Crisis to Public Resource*. Pluto Press.

Merleau Ponty, M. (2012) *The Phenomenology of Perception*. Routledge.

Merryfield, A. (1993) 'Place and space: a Lefebvrian reconciliation', *Transactions of the Institute of British Geographers*, 18(4): 516–531.

Merryfield, A. and Swyngedouw, E. (1996) *The Urbanization of Injustice*. Lawrence and Wishart.

Moran, C. (2013) 'The Riots, Rats and Sad, Silent Queues: My Life under Thatcher', *The Times*, 15 April.

Moran, M. (2006) 'Social Inclusion and the Limits of Pragmatic Liberalism: The Irish Case', *Irish Political Studies*, 21(2): 180–201.

Munck, R. (2007) 'Social Class and Inequality', in O. Sullivan (ed) *Contemporary Ireland: A Sociological Map*. University College Dublin Press.

Norris, M. et al. (2014) *Social Housing Disadvantage and Neighbourhood Liveability: Ten Years of Change in Social Housing Neighbourhoods*. Routledge.

O Byrne, D. (1997) 'Working Class Culture: Local Community and Global Conditions', in J. Eade (ed) *Living the Global: Globalization as Local Process*. Routledge.

O Callaghan, C., Kelly, S., Boyle, M. and Kitchin, R. (2015) 'Topologies and Topographies of Ireland's Neoliberal Crisis', *Space and Polity*, 19(1): 31–46.

O Carroll, A. and Bennett, D. (2017) *The Dublin Docker: Working Lives of Dublin's Deep-Sea Port*. Irish Academic Press.

Olin Wright, E. (1997) *Classes*. Verso.

Olin Wright, E. (2015) *Understanding Class*. Verso.

O Riann, S. (2015) *The Rise and Fall of Ireland's Celtic Tiger: Liberalism, Boom and Bust*. Cambridge University Press.

Parkinson, K. (2016) *The Blocks*. New Binary Press.

Patel, R. and Moore, J.W. (2020) *A History of the World in Seven Cheap Things: A Guide to Capitalism, Nature and the Future of the Planet*. Verso Books.

Pierse, M. (2011) *Writing Ireland's Working Class: Dublin After O'Casey*. Palgrave Macmillan.

Povey, L. (2019) 'Maternal Outcasts: Governing Vulnerable Mothers in Advanced Marginality', in J. Flint and R. Powell (eds) *Class, Ethnicity and State in the Polarized Metropolis: Putting Wacquant to Work*. Palgrave Macmillan, pp 81–106.

Power, A. (1999) *Estates on the Edge: The Social Consequences of Mass Housing in Northern Europe*. Palgrave Macmillan.

Pringle, D.G., Walsh, J. and Hennessy, M. (eds) (1999) *Poor People, Poor Places: A Geography of Poverty and Deprivation in Ireland*. Oak Tree Press.

Ranciere, J. (1991) *The Ignorant Schoolmaster: Five Lessons in Intellectual Emancipation*. Translated and with an introduction by K. Ross. Stanford University Press.

Ranciere, J. (1999) *Disagreement*. University of Minnesota Press.

Ranciere, J. (2012) *Proletarian Nights: The Workers' Dream in Nineteenth Century France*. Verso.

Reay, D. (1998a) 'Rethinking Social Class: Qualitative Perspectives on Class and Gender', *Sociology*, 32(2): 259–275.

Reay, D. (1998b) *Class Work: Mothers Involvement in their Children's Primary Schooling*. UCL Press.

Reay, D. and Lucey, H. (2000) 'I Don't Really Like It Here but I Don't Want to Be Anywhere Else: Children and Inner City Council Estates', *Antipode*, 32(4): 410–428.

Relph, E. (1985) 'Geographical Experiences and Being-in-the-world: The Phenomenological Origins of Geography', in D. Seamon and R. Mugerauer (eds) *Dwelling, Place and Environment: Towards a Phenomenology of Person and World*. Martinus Nijhoff Publishers.

Resnick, S.A. and Wolff, R.D. (1987) *Knowledge and Class: A Marxian Critique of Political Economy*. University of Chicago Press.

Ricoeur, P. (2004) *Memory, History, Forgetting*. Translated by K. Blamey and D. Pellauer. University of Chicago Press.

Ricoeur, P. (2016) *Hermeneutics and the Human Sciences*. Edited and translated by J.B. Thompson. Cambridge Philosophy Classics.

Rogaly, B. and Taylor, B. (2011) *Moving Histories of Class and Community: Identity, Place and Belonging in Contemporary England*. Palgrave Macmillan.

Romyn, M. (2016) 'The Heygate: Community Life in an Inner City Estate: 1974–2011', *History Workshop Journal*, 81: 197–230.

Rosbrook-Thompson, J. and Armstrong, G. (2018) *Mixed-Occupancy Housing in London: A Living Tapestry*. Palgrave Studies in Urban Anthropology.

Ruane, L. (2018) *People Like Me*. Gill Books.

Savage, M. (2015) *Social Class in the 21st Century*. Penguin Classics.

Savage, M. (2021) *The Return of Inequality: Social Change and the Weight of the Past*. Harvard University Press.

Savage, M., Barlow, J., Dickens, P. and Fielding, T. (1992) *Property, Bureaucracy and Culture: Middle Class Formation in Britain*. Routledge.

Savage, M., Devine, F., Cunningham, N., Taylor, M., Yaojun, L., Hjellbreke, J., Le Roux, B., Friedman, S. and Miles, A. (2013) 'A New Model of Social Class: Findings from the BBC's Great British Class Survey Experiment', *Sociology*, 47(2): 219–250.

Sayer, A. (1985) 'The Difference that Space Makes', in D. Gregory, and J. Urry (eds) *Social Relations and Spatial Structures*. Macmillan, pp 49–66.

Sayer, A. (1998) 'Abstraction: A realist interpretation', in M. Archer, R. Bhaskar, A. Collier, T. Lawson and A. Norrie (eds) *Critical Realism Essential Readings*. Centre for Critical Realism. Routledge, pp 120–143.

Sayer, A. (2000) *Realism and Social Science*. Sage Publications.

Sayer, A. (2005) *The Moral Significance of Class*. Cambridge University Press.

Seamon, D. and Mugerauer, R. (1985) *Dwelling, Place and Environment: Towards a Phenomenology of Person and World*. Martinus Mijhoff.

Sennett, R. and Cobb, J. (1993) *The Hidden Injuries of Class*. W.W. Norton & Company.

Sevenhuijsen, S. (1998) *Citizenship and the Ethic of Care*. Routledge.

Shildrick, T. (2018) 'Lessons from Grenfell: Poverty Propaganda, Stigma and Class Power', *The Sociological Review*, 66(4): 783–798.

Silverman, M. (2006) *An Irish Working Class: Explorations in Political Economy and Hegemony, 1800–1950*. Anthropological Horizons, University of Toronto.

Skeggs, B. (2002) *Formations of Class and Gender: Becoming Respectable*. Theory Culture and Society, Sage Publications.

Skeggs, B. (2004) *Class, Self, and Culture*. Routledge.

Soja, E. (1985) 'The Spatiality of Social Life: Towards a Transformative Retheorisation', in D. Gregory and J. Urry (eds) *Social Relations and Spatial Structures*. Macmillan, pp 90–127.

Sperber, D. (1982) 'Apparently Irrational Beliefs', in M. Hollis and S. Lukes (eds) *Rationality and Relativism*. Basil Blackwater Publisher Limited, pp 149–180.

Standing, G. (2011) *The Precariat: The New Dangerous Class*. Bloomsbury.

Steedman, C. (1987) *Landscape for a Good Woman*. Rutgers University Press.

Streeck, W. (2017) *How Will Capitalism End? Essays on a Failing System*. Verso.

Thrift, N. (1996) *Spatial Formations*. First published in association with Theory Culture and Society, School of Human Studies, University of Teeside. Sage Publications.

Tronto, J.C. (1994) *Moral Boundaries: A Political Argument for an Ethic of Care*. Routledge.

Trott, B. (2017) 'Affective Labour and Alienation: Spinoza's Materialism and the Sad Passions of Post-Fordist Work', *Emotion, Space and Society*, 25: 119–126.

Tyler, I. (2008) 'Chav Mum Chav Scum', *Feminist Media Studies* (online, 18 March), http://dx.doi.org./10.1080/14680770701824779.

Umney, C. (2018) *Class Matters: Inequality and Exploitation in 21st Century Britain*. Pluto Press.

UN Special Rapporteur (2018) Statement on a Visit to the United Kingdom, by Professor Philip Alston, United Nations Special Rapporteur on extreme poverty and human rights London, 16 November 2018, www.ohchr.org/en/statements/2018/11/statement-visit-united-kingdom-professor-philip-alston-united-nations-special.

Urry, J. (2000) 'Sociology of Time and Space', in B.S. Turner (ed) *The Blackwell Companion to Social Theory*. Blackwell Publishing, pp 416–443.

Wacquant, L. (2008) *Urban Outcasts: A Comparative* Sociology *of Advanced Marginality*. Polity Press.

Wacquant, L. (2009) *Punishing the Poor: The Neoliberal Government of Social Insecurity*. Duke University Press.

Wacquant, L. (2019) 'Class, Ethnicity and State in the Making of Advanced Marginality', in J. Flint and R. Powell (eds) *Class, Ethnicity and State in the Polarized Metropolis: Putting Wacquant to Work*. Palgrave Macmillan, pp 23–50.

Wallerstein, I. (1983) *Historical Capitalism*. Verso.

Watt, P. (2021) *Estate Regeneration and its Discontents: Public Housing, Place and Inequality in London*. Policy Press.

Weber, M. (1978) *Economy and Society Volume 2*. University of California Press.

Yeung, H. W. (1997) 'Critical Realism and Realist Research in Human Geography', *Progress in Human Geography*, Sage Journals, 21(1): 51–74.

Young, M. and Wilmott, P. (1957) *Family and Kinship in East London*. Pelican Books.

References

Zeleniac, A (2018) 'Lefebvre's Politics of Space: Planning the Urban as Oeuvre', *Urban Planning*, 3(3): 5–15.

Zizek, S. (1989) *The Sublime Object of Ideology*. Verso Books.

Zizek, S. (2009) *Six Sideways Reflections on Violence*. Profile Books.

Index

Index

and production of knowledge 6–7
space, place and ix, 100–101, 119–120, 121–123
class consciousness 28, 102, 103, 104, 106–107
class position, of Bridgetown residents 3–4
clothing 48, 55, 62–63
coal deliveries 72–73
community *see* social interaction; support and solidarity
Conor 30–31
construction industry 25–31, 73, 78–79
conversations with residents 10–11
council officials 20, 21
credit *see* loans and credit
credit unions 59, 60
crime *see* robbery; violence
critical realism 97–99, 129
critical social science 9–10

D

day-to-day activities 11, 45, 97
Debbie 90–91
debt *see* loans and credit; rent arrears
Dee 74
dependency/interdependency 108
see also support and solidarity
deprivation–disadvantage theories 5–6
disability benefit 76, 77, 80
division of labour 40, 111
Doogy 69
drug addiction 67, 71, 93, 94
and disability benefit 77
and ill health 74, 83–84
Rosy's experiences 78, 80, 83–84
treatment clinic 74, 78, 83
drug dealing 66–67
drugs, and violence 65–66

E

economic crash (2008) 25–26, 44, 103
economic resource, estate as 121, 122–123
Eddie 28–29
education
higher education 23
Karl's ambitions 32, 33, 34
schooling 19, 32, 37, 49, 81, 93
embodiment 100, 112, 120, 127–128
Emily 22
emotion, and fragility 75
emotional labour 39–40, 111
emotional work 111
see also affective domain; care work (unpaid)
empirical, in realist theory 98, 99
employment
alongside unpaid care work 20, 110–112
antique furniture removal 79
Charlie 78–79

coal deliveries 72–73
construction industry 25–31, 73, 78–79
factory work 41–42, 82, 84
Frank 25–31, 103–104
health and care sector 19–20, 39–40
hospitality sector 32, 38–39, 73
Karl 32–35
Michelle 20, 36, 38–40
Nadia 41–43
pay and conditions 27–28, 29–31, 34–35, 79, 82, 84, 102–103
retail sector 32–33, 42
Rosy 80–81, 82–83
Steph 84
employment training schemes 19, 36, 43, 79
construction industry 25, 28–29
pre-employment courses 25
Tina's concerns 46, 75–76
youth schemes 82
enunciation 87–88
ethics/morals
concept of 9
expressed in stories and phrases 89–90
'it's not where you live ...' viii, 64, 70–74, 122
'what goes around comes around' 53, 64, 65–69
ethnographic approach 10, 97
eudamonia 9, 129
explanatory critique 10
external goods 3
external relations 7–8

F

factory work 41–42, 82, 84
Fahey, T. 5–6
fairness 50–51
see also 'what goes around comes around'
family, regard for 72
family connections to estate 18, 19, 38, 72
family histories 88, 89
feminist theory 108, 109
fieldwork 10–11
finances *see* money
financial crisis (2008) 25–26, 44, 103
Finn 67, 72–73
food
capital value of 51–52
stories about 88–89
food resources 106
charity food systems 45–53, 106
sharing 43–44, 52–53, 106
'tick' system 43
Foucault, M. 112
fragility 75
Charlie's life trajectory 78–80
Rosy's life trajectory 80–84
Steph's life trajectory 84–85